Here we go again!
Vor dir liegt der Wordmaster.
Er hilft dir beim Wörterlernen.

Sobald du neue Wörter in der Schule besprochen hast, mach die **Words and phrases** in diesem Heft.

Die **fett gedruckten** deutschen Wörter und Ausdrücke sind Lernwörter. Sie fehlen im englischen Satz, damit du sie eintragen kannst.

WORD MASTER

Tipps:

1 Die Reihenfolge der Words and phrases entspricht der Reihenfolge der neuen Wörter im Vocabulary deines Schülerbuches. Dort kannst du deine Lösungen überprüfen.

2 Wenn du mal nicht weiter weißt, kannst du auch im Vocabulary nachschauen.

3 Lerne neue Wörter in einem Satz. So kannst du sie dir besser merken.

1 Words and phrases ➜ (pp. 8–10)

1 You can say "Hi" _____ "Hello". — Du kannst **statt** „Hallo" auch „Hi" sagen.

2 That's not true. It's _____. — Das ist nicht wahr. Es ist **falsch**.

3 "While" and "because" are _____ _____. — „Während" und „weil" sind **Bindewörter**.

4 The _____ of my work is good. — Der **Inhalt** meiner Arbeit ist gut.

Übrigens: Im Anschluss an die **Words and phrases** gibt es kurze Aufgaben, Rätsel und Wortspiele, mit denen du den neuen Wortschatz weiter üben und festigen kannst.

Alle Lösungen findest du in der Mitte des Heftes.

Revision

1 Personal details A–Z

Schreib die Lösungen rechts auf.

1 the word for your mother or father's sister

2 What do you call a school where you sleep?

3 England, France and Germany are ▢.

4 Mum and Dad were married, but they're not now. They're ▢.

5 Someone from England is an ▢ person.

6 What do you call something that makes you laugh?

7 the opposite of "boy"

8 What's the missing word? "▢ birthday!"

9 London is ▢ England.

10 a more informal word for "child"

11 Your home is the place where you ▢.

12 "Dad" is another word for father. What do we say for mother?

13 John, Simon and Tom are all ▢ of boys.

14 To find someone's age you ask "How ▢ are you?"

15 The person you work with is your ▢.

16 a word which is similar to "street"

17 My brother isn't married. He is still ▢.

18 These are children who are born on the same day and look similar.

19 What do you call your father or mother's brother?

20 the opposite of "man"

21 You're not old. You're only ten. That's ▢.

The answers start with the letters A–Z but five letters are missing. Which?

2 Word fields

Schreib die Wörter aus dem Wortspeicher ins passende Wortfeld.

brown · circle · dark · double · green · group · half · large · little ·
long · mile · paper · pink · plastic · purple · rock · rubber · second ·
short · stone · tall · unit · wood · yellow

Colours	Shapes and sizes	Quantities	Materials
_____	_____	_____	_____
_____	_____	_____	_____
_____	_____	_____	_____
_____	_____	_____	_____
_____	_____	_____	_____
_____	_____	_____	_____

3 Scrambled words

Die unterstrichenen Wörter sind alle durcheinander. Schreib sie rechts richtig auf.

1 I wasn't with anyone. I was all **nealo**. _____

2 The children started to run **oscars** the street. _____

3 I sit **dinehb** Jack in class. He is in front of me. _____

4 Monday comes **neteweb** Sunday and Tuesday. _____

5 How **arf** is it from Berlin to London? _____

6 I closed the door and went **diseni** the room. _____

7 We drove slowly because the road was very **wronra**. _____

8 We didn't stop at the shops. We walked straight **spat**. _____

9 I normally put my bag **duenr** my chair. _____

10 We are nearly there. It's just a little **truhref**. _____

4 People and things

Welche Sätze haben eine ähnliche Bedeutung?

1 It wasn't interesting at all.

2 She is brilliant in class.

3 She has no friends.

4 She doesn't find it easy to talk to people.

5 It's great here, far from the noisy city.

6 She doesn't eat meat.

7 She's really looking forward to her party.

8 She has lots of things to do.

9 She's great at football.

10 It was here, but I can't find it now.

11 She looks really unhappy.

12 Saturday and Sunday were perfect.

13 It was awful.

14 It was really difficult.

A She's a vegetarian.

B She's really busy.

C She's a talented player.

D She's excited.

E She is a very clever student.

F I think something has made her sad.

G She is quite lonely.

H It was very boring.

I It was rubbish.

K We had a fantastic weekend.

L She is very shy.

M It was very hard.

N It's really peaceful.

O It's missing.

5 Word fields

In jeder Gruppe passt ein Wort nicht. Streich es durch und schreib es rechts in die Zeile auf, in die es passt.
Finde dann einen passenden Titel für jede Gruppe.

1 clown · dentist · policeman · teacher · designer · tractor · author · director _____

2 drums · guitar · text · piano · concert · instrument · solo · choir _____

3 ticket · ride · roundabout · farmer · minibus · go-kart · ferry · deck _____

4 phone · call · postcard · butterfly · email · message · stamp _____

5 lake · moon · rainforest · recorder · beach · river · summer · valley _____

6 adder · deer · hay · frog · hamster · monkey · shark · worm _____

6 Irregular verbs

Vervollständige die Tabelle mit den richtigen Verbformen.

	Infinitive	Simple past	Past participle
1	blow	_____	blown
2	draw	_____	_____
3	fight	fought	_____
4	know	_____	_____
5	make	made	_____
6	_____	met	met
7	run	_____	run
8	take	_____	taken
9	think	_____	thought
10	understand	understood	_____

7 True or false?

Sind die Aussagen wahr oder falsch?

	True	False
1 "The" and "an" are articles.	◯	◯
2 You should end a sentence with a comma.	◯	◯
3 There are two syllables in the word "theme".	◯	◯
4 "Friendly" is an adverb.	◯	◯
5 B, S, T and W are all consonants.	◯	◯
6 A paragraph is normally shorter than a sentence.	◯	◯
7 The endings of "guessed" and "best" sound the same.	◯	◯
8 When you open a dictionary, it is an "entry".	◯	◯
9 Sometimes you make questions by changing the word order of a sentence.	◯	◯
10 There are no hyphens or colons in this English sentence.	◯	◯

8 Crossword

Trag die englischen Übersetzungen der deutschen Wörter ins Gitter ein.

Across →

2 Wanduhr
5 Kästchen
7 Meister
8 Schild
11 Arm
12 Hund
14 Katze
16 Nase
17 Boot
19 Kirche
23 Gitarre
25 Preis
26 Arzt
30 Zunge
32 Messer
33 Fußball

Down ↓

1 Milch
3 Stuhl
4 Tanz
5 Brücke
6 Garten
7 Fotoapparat
9 Nacken
10 Tasche
13 Turm
15 Zähne
17 Glocke
18 Finger
20 Haar
21 Füße
22 Fahrkarte
24 Bein
26 Schreibtisch
27 Ei
28 Herz
29 Vogel
31 Schüssel

9 Wrong weather!

Verbessere den Schreibfehler in jedem Satz. Schreib das richtige Wort rechts auf.

1 The temperatur has changed. It is colder today than yesterday. _____

2 We saw flashes of lightening several times during the storm. _____

3 You need your umbrella. It's a very raining day. _____

4 Did you hear the tunder last night? It was very loud. _____

5 It's was a lot cooler than we expected here last autumn. _____

6 What do you think the wheather will be like tomorrow? _____

7 Was that a flesh of lightning? _____

8 I like it when the it's hot and sonny. _____

9 I can't see anything in this misst. _____

10 There's a lot of sno on the mountains this month. _____

10 Join the sentences

Verbinde die beiden Satzteile, um sinnvolle Sätze zu bilden.

1 The first pet I had was a guinea   A tennis before we went for lunch.

2 There should be a question   B artist in the town centre yesterday.

3 For homework we had to draw our family   C pool in the garden.

4 My big brother works as a shop   D call to tell them I was a bit late.

5 It's a great hotel. There's a swimming   E pig called Harold.

6 We had a quick game of table   F mark here because you're asking why.

7 There was a brilliant street   G assistant at the weekend.

8 I made a quick phone   H tree and prepare a presentation on it.

11 The fourth word

Vervollständige die Lücken mit einem vierten Wort.

1

win	winner
listen	_____

2

bike	ride
mountain	_____

3

author	book
singer	_____

4

play	player
swim	_____

5

yacht	boat
tulip	_____

6

give	take
turn on	_____

7

man	hand
dog	_____

8

prince	princess
king	_____

9

possible	impossible
always	_____

10

me	mine
our	_____

11

child	children
tooth	_____

12

celebration	celebrate
invitation	_____

12 Compound nouns

Verbinde ein Wortteil aus Spalte 1 mit einem aus Spalte 2, um ein zusammengesetztes Wort zu bilden.
Schreib es rechts auf.

1	2	Compound noun
appoint	appear	_____
back	bour	_____
class	ener	_____
dis	ground	_____
grand	light	_____
high	mate	_____
neigh	ment	_____
sharp	parents	_____
time	table	_____

1 Unit

This is London

1 Words and phrases ➔ (pp. 8–10)

1 The _____ _____ _____ my holidays was London: it's a _____ and very interesting city.	Das **Beste an** meinen Ferien war London: Es ist eine **riesige** und sehr interessante Stadt.
2 I want to go back _____ _____ ____ I can.	Ich will, **sobald** ich kann, zurück.
3 The _____ was fantastic.	Der **Dom** war fantastisch.
4 We didn't have time to see the _____.	Wir hatten keine Zeit, den **Palast** zu besuchen.
5 A group of tourists were speaking _____.	Eine Gruppe Touristen haben **Walisisch** gesprochen.
6 They _____ ____ my questions in English.	Sie **antworteten auf** meine Fragen auf Englisch.
7 Lots of tourists were from _____ _____.	Viele Touristen waren aus **Westeuropa**.
8 How do you open this camera? Ah, _____.	Wie macht man diese Kamera auf? Ach, **verstehe**.
9 We took the _____ to the 20th floor.	Wir nahmen den **Fahrstuhl** in den 20. Stock.
10 The view is _____. There's the palace.	Die Aussicht ist **unglaublich**. Da ist der Palast.
11 – _____ do you know? Maybe it's a hotel.	– **Woher** weißt du das? Vielleicht ist es ein Hotel.
12 – No, I saw a photo in a _____ today.	– Nein, ich sah heute ein Foto in einem **Blog-Eintrag**.

2 Q & A

Verbinde die Fragen mit der richtigen Antwort.

1 The Queen doesn't live in a normal house, right?

2 Was the hotel big or small?

3 What's that? A church?

4 Are they English?

5 It's on the top floor. Are we taking the stairs?

6 So what did you do when he asked the question?

7 So, how was your holiday?

8 Are you going to see your grandma tomorrow?

a No, a cathedral.

b No, Welsh.

c I replied.

d No, but as soon as I can.

e No, a palace.

f Huge.

g No. The lift!

h Amazing, thanks.

3 Words and phrases → (pp. 10–12)

1 _____ is in March this year.	**Fasching** ist dieses Jahr im März.
2 We had a grammar _____ in English today.	Heute hatten wir in Englisch einen Grammatik**test**.
3 I _____ really _____ sport, but not cricket.	Ich **stehe** echt **auf** Sport, aber nicht Cricket.
4 I really _____ football matches.	Ich **genieße** Fußballspiele sehr.
5 _____, I've got tickets for the match.	**Übrigens**: Ich habe zwei Karten für das Spiel.
6 My friend lives in the _____ of the country.	Mein Freund wohnt im **Süden** des Landes.
7 There was no light: I enjoyed the _____.	Es gab kein Licht: Ich habe die **Finsternis** genossen.
8 Guess what I'm thinking of. Here's a _____.	Rate mal, woran ich denke. Hier ist ein **Hinweis**.
9 The New York _____ is very famous.	Die **Skyline** von New York ist sehr berühmt.
10 That's not true. It's _____.	Das ist nicht wahr. Es ist **falsch**.
11 Holidays and homework don't _____ _____.	Ferien und Hausaufgaben **passen** nicht **zusammen**.
12 Did you see the Queen _____ the _____?	Hast du die Königin **in der U-Bahn** gesehen?
13 What do you call the London _____?	Wie nennt man die Londoner **U-Bahn**?
14 It costs a lot to _____ ____ this hotel.	Es kostet viel, **in** diesem Hotel zu **übernachten**.
15 We saw a _____ outside the _____.	Wir sahen einen **Fahrplan** vor der **Galerie**.
16 We ate in a nice _____ in the evening.	Abends aßen wir in einem netten **Restaurant**.

4 What are they describing?

Was beschreiben die Leute? Schreib das Wort rechts neben die Erklärung.

1 You need this to know when the trains and buses leave. _____

2 If you don't want to eat at home you go here. _____

3 When you can't see because there's no light, you are in this. _____

4 This is where you can see fantastic paintings. _____

5 When you write a new entry on a blog, this is what you write. _____

6 This is what they call the underground in London. _____

7 It's not true. _____

8 The sight of the tops of skyscrapers and tall buildings of a city. _____

5 Words and phrases ➜ (pp. 13–14)

*This is true!
Please say BerLIN.

1 The _____ is on the second syllable of "Berlin".*	Die **Betonung** liegt auf der zweiten Silbe von „Berlin".
2 Good dictionaries show _____.	Gute Wörterbücher zeigen **Betonungszeichen** an.
3 I'm not good at _____.	Ich bin nicht gut in **spontan geführten Gesprächen**.
4 What's the best way to enjoy _____?	Wie genießt man am besten **Kultur**?
5 When I ask a question, I _____ an answer.	Wenn ich eine Frage stelle, **erwarte** ich eine Antwort.
6 You can't see all the _____ in one day.	Du kannst nicht alle **Attraktionen** an einem Tag sehen.
7 Are you interested in _____?	Interessierst du dich für **Naturkunde**?
8 It's great that _____ to many museums is free.	Es ist toll, dass der **Eintritt** in viele Museen kostenlos ist.
9 I like that about _____.	Das mag ich an **dem Vereinigten Königreich**.
10 Would you like to _____ a table?	Möchten Sie einen Tisch **reservieren**?
11 – Er, we have already, _____.	– Äh, haben wir **eigentlich** schon.
12 Tell me an interesting _____ about Berlin.	Erzähl mir einen interessanten **Fakt** über Berlin.
13 – OK, the TV tower has 986 _____!	– Also, der Fernsehturm hat 986 **Stufen**!
14 – If you have the _____, you must go.	– Wenn du die **Gelegenheit** hast, musst du hin.

6 Missing words

Schreib die drei fehlenden Wörter in die richtige Lücke.

season · syllable · evening · big · stress · entry · call · country · enjoy · fact · History · felt · good · small · culture · Europe · reserve · ticket · way · thing · sport · free · time · well

1 The _____ on _____ is on the first _____.

2 You don't need a _____ to the museum because _____ is _____.

3 I made a phone _____ to _____ a table for later the same _____.

4 Each _____ in _____ has its own _____, and they are all a bit different.

5 The best _____ about our _____ in London was the Natural _____ museum.

6 I'm not into _____, but I _____ music. So does my dad, by the _____.

7 It can make a _____ difference if you are _____ at _____ talk.

8 Unfortunately, I wasn't _____. I _____ terrible, in _____.

7 Words and phrases → *(p. 15)*

1 History is more than just facts and _____.	Geschichte ist mehr als nur Fakten und **Zahlen**.
2 There's _____ to do on Friday _____ on Monday.	Es gibt **weniger** am Freitag zu tun **als** am Montag.
3 I'd like a _____ more than a dog.	Ich hätte lieber eine **Schildkröte** als einen Hund.
4 We put the books _____.	Wir haben die Bücher **aufeinander** gelegt.
5 We saw _____ when we were on the bus.	Wir sahen das **Parlament**, als wir im Bus saßen.
6 Mum can do 2 things _____. Dad can't.	Mama kann 2 Sachen **gleichzeitig** tun, Papa nicht.
7 Do you celebrate _____?	Feiert ihr **Weihnachten**?
8 We got our tickets from the _____.	Wir haben unsere Karten von der **Kasse** abgeholt.
9 I'll tell you another _____ later.	Ich erzähle dir später eine weitere **Einzelheit**.
10 An _____ pays more than a child.	Ein **Erwachsener** zahlt mehr als ein Kind.
11 What's the entry for a _____ ____ _____?	Was kostet der Eintritt für eine **elfköpfige Familie**?
12 We asked lots of questions _____ the tour.	Wir haben **während** der Tour viele Fragen gestellt.
13 The men who _____ the tower know a lot.	Die Männer, die den Turm **bewachen**, wissen viel.
14 The _____ eat biscuits made of _____!	Die **Raben** fressen Kekse aus **Blut**!
15 The Tower ____ _____ ____ the Crown _____.	Der Tower **beheimatet** die Kron**juwelen**.

8 The fourth word

Wie lautet das vierte Wort? Schreib es in die rechte Spalte.

1 east – west   north – _____

2 wrong – right   false – _____

3 house – palace   church – _____

4 teeth – white   blood – _____

5 young – old   children – _____

6 many – few   more – _____

7 football – sport   raven – _____

8 day – night   light – _____

9 home – live   hotel – _____

9 Words and phrases → (p. 16)

1 You can say "Hi" _____ "Hello".	Du kannst **statt** „Hallo" auch „Hi" sagen.
2 We're leaving soon. On Thursday, to be _____.	Wir fahren bald. Am Donnerstag, um **genau** zu sein.
3 "While" and "because" are _____ _____.	„Während" und „weil" sind **Bindewörter**.
4 We call them that because they _____ sentences.	Wir nennen sie so, weil sie Sätze **verbinden**.
5 There was a big _____ at the ticket office.	Es gab eine lange **Schlange** vor der Kasse.
6 The film was €20. It was _____ about 20 cents.	Der Film kostete €20. Er war ungefähr 20 Cent **wert**.
7 We were near the zoo. A lion _____ _____.	Wir waren in der Nähe des Zoos. Ein Löwe **hat gebrüllt**.
8 The zoo is always _____ at the weekend.	Der Zoo ist am Wochenende immer **voller Menschen**.

10 Missing words

Vervollständige die E-Mail mit diesen Wörtern:

birthday · biscuits · blood · Christmas · during · famous · figures · guard · instead · interesting · into · jewels · office · one · Parliament · ravens · steps · surprised

To:

Subject: Our trip to London

At **1** _____ we went to London. Dad is really **2** _____ history –

his head is full of facts and **3** _____, so he loved learning about the number

of **4** _____ inside Big Ben, how many people can go up in the London Eye

at **5** _____ time, and he read all about the **6** _____ people who have been

in **7** _____. I like stories, so it was **8** _____ to hear about

the **9** _____ at the Tower from the Beefeaters, who **10** _____ the place.

Mum was **11** _____ that the birds eat **12** _____ that are made of

13 _____. She loved the Crown **14** _____ that we saw **15** _____ our

visit there, and asked Dad if she could have some for her **16** _____. He said he

didn't have much money left after the price he paid at the ticket **17** _____, but

he could take us to a nice restaurant **18** _____ _____ that, if we wanted.

11 Words and phrases ➔ *(pp. 17–18)*

1 I got good _____ on my idea. | Ich bekam eine gute **Rückmeldung** zu meiner Idee.

2 I'm sure it'll help me _____ my work. | Ich bin sicher, dass es meine Arbeit **verbessern** wird.

3 That's how I should _____ ____ feedback. | So sollte ich **auf** Feedback **reagieren**.

4 The _____ of my work is good, Dad said. | Der **Inhalt** meiner Arbeit ist gut, hat Papa gesagt.

5 But he told me how to _____ ideas better. | Aber er sagte mir, wie man Ideen besser **verbindet**.

6 And he _____ _____ some mistakes ____ _____. | Und er **hat mich** auf einige Fehler **hingewiesen**.

7 Three different _____ go to Oxford Circus. | Drei verschiedene **Linien** führen zum Oxford Circus.

8 Do I go _____ or _____? | Fahre ich **Richtung Norden** oder **Richtung Süden**?

9 You don't have to _____: it's just one stop. | Du musst nicht **umsteigen**: Es ist nur eine Station.

12 Wrong!

Verbessere die zwei Schreibfehler in jedem Satz. Schreibe die korrigierten Wörter rechts auf.

1 I got very usful fedback on the project I did for homework. _____ _____

2 For exampel, I should use linking words to conect ideas. _____ _____

3 There were also sum speling mistakes to correct. _____ _____

4 I think my english is really improuving. _____ _____

5 Do we need the soutbound or northbund line? _____ _____

6 The galery was free, but there was a long kue to get in. _____ _____

7 Crowds and popular atractions go togeter, unfortunately. _____ _____

8 It cost £10.50, to be exakt, but I think it was wert more. _____ _____

13 Words and phrases → (pp. 19–20)

1 I was late because my watch _____ _____.	Ich kam zu spät, weil meine Uhr **nachging**.
2 It just _____ _____ at the moment.	Zurzeit **funktioniert** sie einfach **nicht**.
3 Let's _____ _____ the shops at the weekend.	Lass uns am Wochenende **auf** die Läden **zusteuern**.
4 I have a very important _____.	Ich habe eine sehr wichtige **Ansage**.
5 What is the _____ of this book for you?	Was ist für dich die **Botschaft** dieses Buchs?
6 We were the only people on the _____.	Wir waren die einzigen auf dem **Bahnsteig**.
7 My favourite programme ____ _____ tonight.	Meine Lieblingssendung **läuft** heute Abend.
8 I want a new watch, but Dad says: "_____!"	Ich will eine neue Uhr, aber Papa sagt: „**Auf keinen Fall!**"
9 I've wanted a new one _____ weeks.	Ich will eine neue schon **seit** Wochen.
10 I've had the old one _____ 2006!	Ich habe meine alte **seit** 2006!
11 "The old one still works. _____ _____, you have enough money to buy your own," he says.	Er sagt: „Die alte funktioniert noch. **Und überhaupt**, du hast genug Geld, um dir eine eigene zu kaufen."
12 Oh well, it was worth a _____.	Na ja, es war einen **Versuch** wert.

14 Join the parts

Verbinde die Wortteile und vervollständige die Sätze mit den Wörtern.

1 My pet is really slow. It's a ████. _____

2 The ████ said the train was 15 minutes late. _____

3 What did the artist want to say? What was his ████? _____

4 I didn't buy it because it was expensive. And ████, I didn't need it. _____

5 We were standing on the ████ and waiting for the train. _____

6 She said the museum was special, but didn't give any ████. _____

7 The teacher told us to check that the ████ of our work was right. _____

8 It was a surprise, so I didn't know what to ████. _____

15 Words and phrases ➜ *(pp. 20–21)*

1 I want to watch a film.	Ich will einen Film sehen.
Where's the _____ _____?	Wo ist die **Fernbedienung**?
2 Please _____ the TV _____ – I can't hear anything.	**Stell** den Fernseher bitte **lauter** – ich kann nichts hören.
3 The two men didn't talk to _____ _____.	Die zwei Männer haben nicht mit**einander** geredet.
4 They just sat in the _____ and watched TV.	Sie saßen bloß in der **Kneipe** und sahen fern.
5 Nothing happened _____ __ _____.	Nichts passierte **eine Zeit lang**.
6 Then one man felt a _____ on his shoulder.	Dann spürte ein Mann ein **Klopfen** an seiner Schulter.
7 "_____ _____ ____ _____," his wife said.	„**Ab mit dir jetzt**," sagte seine Ehefrau.
8 He walked slowly _____ the door.	Er ging langsam **auf** die Tür **zu**.
9 That story was in the simple past _____.	Die Geschichte war im **Tempus** Präteritum.
10 The story _____ ____ for a long time. I fell asleep.	Die Geschichte **war** lange **im Gange**. Ich schlief ein.
11 I've never been in a _____ like this before.	In solch einer **Situation** war ich noch nie.

16 Scrambled story

Verbinde die Texte so, dass sie eine Geschichte ergeben.

A I'm really into sport. One of the best things about my school

G I was very young. I went there with a friend for

D in my town once or twice a week since

E is that it gives us a chance to play a lot of sport – football, cricket

B often crowded on Saturdays and Sundays.

C tennis and more. My favourite sport is swimming.

F an hour yesterday, in fact. The problem is that it is

H I've always enjoyed it, and have been to the swimming pool

Answer:

17 Words and phrases → *(pp. 22–24)*

1 Each bus has a different _____ through the city. | Jeder Bus hat eine andere **Route** durch die Stadt.

2 The _____ of the buses is also different. | Die **Geschwindigkeit** der Busse ist auch verschieden.

3 _____ __ _____ that it rained during the carnival. | **Es ist schade**, dass es während des Karnevals regnete.

4 "_____ _____ _____ my arm," Mum said to me. | „**Halte dich an** meinem Arm **fest**," sagte mir Mama.

5 She _____ the street _____ her dog. | Sie **suchte** die Straße **nach** ihrem Hund **ab**.

6 Crowds _____ the streets at the weekend. | Menschenmengen **füllen** die Straßen am Wochenende.

7 It's hard to walk along the _____. | Es ist schwer, auf dem **Bürgersteig** zu laufen.

Rocky!!

18 Missing words

In jeder Zeile fehlt ein Wort in *einer* der Lücken. Schreib das Wort auf.

1 I'd like to **a** — visit, but I don't think I'd like to live in **b** *the* UK.

2 I sent a reply to her **a** _____ text message as soon **b** _____ possible.

3 The books are on top **a** _____ each other **b** _____ in the corner of the room.

4 At the end of the lesson the teacher **a** _____ said "Off **b** _____ go now".

5 Why don't we go outside and **a** _____ play football instead **b** _____ watching TV?

6 My friend said we have a test in school **a** _____ tomorrow, but how **b** _____ he know?

7 It's **a** _____ pity you can't come with us to the carnival **b** _____ next week.

8 Hold **a** _____ to your hats! The wind is **b** _____ really strong.

9 I need to relax for **a** _____ while. I'm **b** _____ feeling quite tired.

10 The guide pointed **a** _____ the attractions during **b** _____ our tour of the city.

19 Words and phrases → (pp. 24–25)

1 City maps are _____ in many shops.	Stadtpläne sind in vielen Läden **erhältlich**.
2 The shops are _____ _____ the town centre.	Die Läden sind **überall um** das Stadtzentrum **herum**.
3 He looked at his watch and took a _____ out.	Er schaute auf die Uhr und nahm eine **Pfeife** heraus.
4 He _____ his _____. The game was over.	Er **pfiff**. Das Spiel war vorbei.
5 I couldn't find my phone and _____.	Ich fand mein Handy nicht und **geriet in Panik**.
6 I don't know _____ where I lost it.	Ich weiß nicht **genau**, wo ich es verloren habe.
7 I _____ _____ and went under the _____.	Ich **bückte mich** und ging unter das **Seil**.
8 Butterfly _____ can be like a _____.	Schmetterlings**flügel** können wie ein **Regenbogen** sein.
9 If I turn around too fast, I get _____.	Wenn ich mich zu schnell umdrehe, wird mir **schwindlig**.
10 Move your _____ – that's how _____ dance.	Bewege deine **Hüften** – so tanzt **man**.
11 You need to follow the _____ too.	Man muss auch dem **Rhythmus** folgen.
12 The _____ _____ me.	Der **Lautsprecher hat** mich **erschreckt**.
13 _____ you _____ if I _____ here?	**Hast** du **was dagegen**, wenn ich **mich** hier **ausruhe**?
14 There was _____ _____ _____ my family at home.	Es gab zu Hause **keine Spur von** meiner Familie.
15 "Oh no," I said _____ _____ _____.	„Ach nein", sagte ich **flüsternd**.

20 True or false

Sind die Aussagen wahr oder falsch?   True False

1 Dogs and cats have legs; cows and horses have wings.

2 If your friend is not available, it means you can't talk to him.

3 You feel calm when you panic.

4 You have more than one hip.

5 You can see rainbows in the sky after rain.

6 People feel scared when they are happy.

7 If you say something under your breath, you don't want people to hear.

8 "Rest" and "relax" are very different.

2 Unit

Welcome to Snowdonia

1 Words and phrases ➜ (p. 30)

1 The house was quiet because it was _____ .	Das Haus war leise, weil es **leer** war.
2 _____ _____ our world.	**Naturwissenschaftler untersuchen** unsere Welt.
3 Dad needs a _____ : he's a _____ .	Papa braucht eine **Werkstatt**: Er ist **Tischler**.
4 His _____ beautiful.	Seine **Möbel sind** schön.
5 I like smelling _____ on a _____ ____ wood.	Ich mag es, **Öl** an einem **Stück** Holz zu riechen.
6 I want to hang a picture up. Where's my _____ ?	Ich will ein Bild aufhängen. Wo ist mein **Hammer**?
7 Some friends are _____ _____ this evening.	Freunde **kommen** heute Abend **vorbei**.
8 Is it fun to _____ _____ ____ someone?	Macht es Spaß, **sich über** Leute **lustig** zu **machen**?
9 The first rule of life is: don't _____ ____ !	Die erste Regel des Lebens lautet: Nicht **aufgeben**!
10 What are your plans for _____ ?	Was sind deine Pläne für **heute Nacht**?

2 Match the parts

Verbinde die Sätze links
mit den Aussagen rechts.
Bilde Dialoge.

1 I'd love to walk on the moon.

2 His dad cuts hair. Did you know?

3 He's very good at art.

4 I love working with wood.

5 Can you play the piano and the guitar?

6 Is your brother a teacher?

7 What do you call someone who plans houses?

8 Does your dad wear a uniform?

a You should be a carpenter.

b No, he's a scientist.

c An architect.

d Really? He's a hairdresser?

e You can if you are an astronaut.

f Yes, his parents are painters.

g Yes. I'm a musician.

h Yes, he's a policeman.

3 Words and phrases → (pp. 31–32)

1 I love buildings. I want to be an _____.	Ich liebe Gebäude. Ich will **Architektin** werden.
2 When I was five I wanted to be an _____.	Als ich fünf war, wollte ich **Astronaut** werden.
3 How often do you go to the _____?	Wie oft gehst du zum **Friseur**?
4 He's a _____. Maybe you know his songs.	Er ist **Musiker**. Vielleicht kennst du seine Lieder.
5 A _____ is painting our flat tomorrow.	Ein **Maler** streicht morgen unsere Wohnung.
6 What do you do for the _____ _____?	Was machst du für die **Natur**?
7 There's information about each _____.	Es gibt Informationen über jedes **Stichwort**.
8 You can see what _____ it is.	Du kannst sehen, welche **Wortart** es ist.
9 Some dictionaries give a _____.	Einige Wörterbucher geben eine **Übersetzung** an.
10 You normally find _____ _____.	Man findet normalerweise **Kohle unter der Erde**.
11 Mum has _____ me this week.	Mama hat mir diese Woche **Hausarrest erteilt**.
12 The _____ sent us an _____ letter.	Die **Beamtin** hat uns einen **amtlichen** Brief geschickt.
13 The _____ round here _____ very friendly.	Die **Polizei** hier in der Gegend **ist** sehr freundlich.

4 Come and look

Vervollständige diese Mini-Dialoge mit *come* oder *look*
und einem (oder zwei) Wörtern aus dem Kasten:

> across · after · around · down · forward ·
> into · over · to · up (3 x) · with (2 x)

1 Have the police found your mum's car yet? → No, they're still _____ing _____ it.

2 I can't think of anything fun to do at the weekend. → Don't worry, I'm sure you'll _____ ____ _____ something.

3 I don't understand what this means. → Then _____ it _____ in a dictionary.

4 Can I visit you again next week? → Yes, why not _____ _____ on Thursday?

5 What was the best thing about your holiday in Wales? → It was lovely to _____ _____ a little mountain lake.

6 Why isn't Philip here? → His mum says he's _____ _____ _____ something.

7 Why were you scared? → I _____ed _____ from my book and there was a ghost!

8 So, Tom is going to the USA. → Yes, he's _____ing _____ _____ New York.

9 You have a beautiful garden. → Thanks, would you like to _____ _____?

10 You're going on holiday next week, right? → Yes, could you maybe _____ _____ our cat?

5 Words and phrases → (p. 34)

*Germany has 15 too.

1 There are 15 _____ parks in Britain.*	Es gibt 15 **National**parks in Großbritannien.
2 He has £5, and I have £3, so £8 _____.	Er hat £5, und ich habe £3, also **insgesamt** £8.
3 A _____ is not the same as a hotel.	Eine **Jugendherberge** ist nicht das gleiche wie ein Hotel.
4 I _____ what the view is like from the top.	Ich **frage mich**, wie der Ausblick von oben ist.
5 They _____ to be poor, but they're rich.	Sie **tun so, als ob** sie arm sind, aber sie sind reich.
6 "I don't understand." – "_____."	„Ich verstehe nicht." – „**Ich auch nicht**."
7 Our holiday _____ _____ so quickly.	Unser Urlaub **ging** so schnell **vorbei**.
8 Be careful. Don't do anything _____.	Sei vorsichtig. Mach nichts **Dummes**.
9 He jumped in and swam _____.	Er sprang hinein und schwamm **flussabwärts**.
10 Don't put the glass so near the _____ of the table.	Stell das Glas nicht so nah an die Tisch**kante**.
11 We'll _____ London before the show starts.	Wir **erreichen** London, bevor die Show anfängt.
12 I saw a _____ and _____ it.	Ich habe einen **Stock** gesehen und **schnappte** ihn **mir**.

6 Which verb?

Wähle das richtige Verb aus, um die Sätze zu vervollständigen, und schreibe es rechts auf.

1 When you feel bored, the hours **come** · **go** by very slowly. _____

2 It's not nice to **do** · **make** fun of people. _____

3 Some friends are **coming** · **going** over to our house tonight. _____

4 They're late. I **ask** · **wonder** where they are. _____

5 Have you lost something? What are you **looking** · **seeing** for? _____

6 Our car wasn't working and we didn't **grab** · **reach** home until the next day. _____ _____

7 She's wonderful. I've never **come** · **been** across anyone like her before. _____

8 Don't stop now. You can do it. Don't **take** · **give** up. _____

7 Words and phrases → *(pp. 35–37)*

1 The last part of the mountain was very _____.	Das letzte Stück des Berges war sehr **steil**.
2 I started singing, and my friend _____ _____.	Ich fing an zu singen und mein Freund **sang mit**.
3 Even the teachers _____ ____.	Sogar die Lehrer **machten mit**.
4 _____ _____ everyone was singing.	**Schon bald** sangen alle.
5 Dad _____ her _____ ____ go out at night.	Papa **forderte** sie **auf**, nachts **nicht** auszugehen.
6 This is your last _____. Don't do that again.	Das ist deine letzte **Warnung**: Mach das nie wieder.
7 I'd love to be a _____ actor.	Ich würde so gerne **Film**schauspieler sein.
8 Our _____ _____ makes the rules.	Unsere **Schulleiterin** macht die Regeln.
9 She doesn't _____ us to use mobiles at break.	Sie **erlaubt** uns nicht, Handys in der Pause zu benutzen.

8 So much stress

In jeder Gruppe Knochen sind drei der neun Wörter falsch am Platz, weil sie anders betont werden.
Streich die falschen durch und schreib sie in die richtige Knochensammlung.

wonder · tonight · allow · hostel · movie · enough · teacher · national · workshop

warning · police · pretend · empty · stupid · alone · before · along · across

Stress on the
first syllable ['--]

Stress on the
second syllable [-'-]

9 Missing letters

In jeder Zeile fehlt einem Wort ein Buchstabe. Schreib das Wort in der richtigen Schreibweise rechts auf.

1 How many people went to the party altogeter? _____

2 My friend doesn't like flying. Me either. _____

3 Mines are places where people work undergrund. _____

4 I sat on the ege of the river and wondered where I was. _____

5 The carpenter put some ol on the new furniture. _____

6 I would like to be a sientist when I am older. _____

10 Words and phrases ➜ *(p. 38)*

1 Which is the _____ _____?	Welcher ist der **Satz, der in das Thema einführt**?
2 Berlin and Hamburg are _____ by water.	Berlin und Hamburg sind durch Wasserwege **verbunden**.
3 We write _____ and say three _____ five.	Wir schreiben **3,5** und sagen drei **Komma** fünf.
4 It was a long _____ to the _____.	Es war ein langer **Aufstieg** bis zum **Gipfel**.
5 It was over _____ m, but I _____ it.	Er war über **1 000** m, aber ich **habe** es **geschafft**.
6 I ate something, then _____ my climb.	Ich aß etwas, dann **setzte** ich meinen Aufstieg **fort**.
7 The way _____ was quicker than the climb.	Der Weg **bergab** war schneller als der Aufstieg.
8 You need _____ to do things like that.	Du brauchst **Energie**, um solche Dinge zu machen.
9 I was walking for ___ _____ ____ eight hours.	Ich lief **insgesamt** acht Stunden.
10 Then I ate a _____ of chocolate. I'm a _____!	Dann aß ich eine **Tafel** Schokolade. Ich bin ein **Held**!
11 I _____ my text and improved it.	Ich **überarbeitete** und verbesserte meinen Text.
12 I _____ my ideas and _____ more.	Ich **organisierte** meine Ideen und **fügte** weitere **hinzu**.

11 Make pairs

Verbinde die Teile, um sinnvolle Paare zu bilden.
(Auf einer Kopie kannst du die Teile ausschneiden. Wenn alles richtig ist, erhältst du eine geometrische Figur.)

12 Words and phrases ➜ *(pp. 39–40)*

1 This isn't easy. In fact, it's very _____.

Das ist nicht einfach. Eigentlich ist sehr **schwierig**.

2 Dad made a yummy apple and _____ salad.

Papa stellte einen leckeren Apfel-**Mohrrüben**-Salat her.

3 Please _____ "1" to hear the message again.

Bitte „1" **drücken**, um die Nachricht nochmal zu hören.

4 We _____ went to bed at 2 am.

Wir gingen um 2 Uhr **endlich** ins Bett.

5 He _____ not _____ to eat during the _____.

Er **war** nicht **in der Lage**, während der **Mahlzeit** zu essen.

6 I _____ _____ the same mistakes.

Ich **mache immer wieder** die gleichen Fehler.

7 I walked _____ along the _____.

Ich ging **lautlos** den **Gang** entlang.

8 Aren't the _____ _____ tonight?

Sind die **Sterne** heute Abend nicht **zauberhaft**?

9 Mum had to _____ _____. She was very tired.

Mama musste **sich hinlegen**. Sie war sehr müde.

10 It's too _____ here. I need to go out.

Es ist mir zu **hektisch** hier. Ich muss raus.

11 Please help me to _____ the table.

Hilf mir bitte, den Tisch **abzuräumen**.

12 There was a nice _____ from the sea.

Eine schöne **Brise** kam vom Meer.

13 Please _____ __ _____ ____ my story.

Wirf bitte **einen Blick auf** meine Geschichte.

14 She _____ _____ when she heard the phone.

Sie **setzte sich auf**, als sie das Telefon hörte.

15 Do you like _____ or plastic toys more?

Magst du **Holz**- oder Kunststoffspielzeuge lieber?

16 My eyes opened _____

Meine Augen öffneten sich **weit**,

when I saw the _____.

als ich die **Gestalt** sah.

13 Word groups

Schreibe die Wörter aus dem Kasten in die richtige Spalte der Tabelle. Welche Wörter passen in keine der Spalten?

breeze · cathedral · coal · director · dizzy · gallery · head teacher · official · pavement · police · pub · rainbow · scientist · spelling · star · summit · underground

Things in a city	The natural world	The world of work

14 Words and phrases → (p. 41)

1 After the first four _____, we all knew the song.	Nach den ersten vier **Noten** kannten wir alle das Lied.
2 Today is _____ ___ nice day. The weather is ____ nice.	Heute ist **so ein** schöner Tag. Das Wetter ist **so** schön.
3 Did it happen, or _____ he _____ it ____?	Ist es geschehen, oder **hat** er **sich** es **ausgedacht**?
4 If they can't agree, they _____.	Wenn sie sich nicht einigen können, **streiten** sie **sich**.
5 That looks delicious. Can I try a _____?	Das sieht lecker aus. Kann ich einen **Bissen** probieren?
6 The _____ looks after the hostel.	Die **Leiterin** passt auf das Wohnheim auf.
7 We went to her _____ to say goodbye.	Wir sind zu ihr ins **Büro** gegangen, um Tschüs zu sagen.

15 Almost the same

Verbinde die Sätze, die eine ähnliche Bedeutung haben.

1 There are too many people in the kitchen.	a It was quite narrow.
2 Is "tonight" a noun or verb, or something different?	b I'm going to continue.
3 The car went at such a speed! It was great.	c It's true. It really happened.
4 We sat there silently.	d What part of speech is it?
5 It was nice because of the breeze.	e It's very busy there.
6 The road was not very wide.	f I have to be in bed early.
7 He pretended he was angry.	g What's the translation?
8 I want to keep playing. It's fun.	h There was a nice little wind.
9 It wasn't easy, but I was able to find a solution.	i We didn't make any noise.
10 My parents don't allow me stay up so late.	j I managed to do it.
11 How do you say that in German?	k We drove very fast.
12 I promise: I didn't make it up	l He shouted, but he was just acting.

16 Words and phrases ➜ (p. 42)

*About 500 teams play in Germany. Look for one near you at *jugger.org*.

1 Do you know _____ _____ play "Jugger"?*	Weißt du, **wie man** „Jugger" spielt?
2 It's so strange, I don't know _____ _____ say.	Es ist so seltsam, dass ich nicht weiß, **was** ich sagen **soll**.
3 He's not sure _____ _____ go for the holidays.	Er ist nicht sicher, **wohin** er in Urlaub fahren **soll**.
4 Do you know _____ _____ ask?	Weißt du, **wen** man fragen **sollte**?
5 I always have to _____ when I visit Grandma.	Ich muss **mich** immer **benehmen**, wenn ich Oma besuche.
6 I took a _____ and started to _____ the floor.	Ich nahm einen **Mopp** und fing an, den Boden zu **wischen**.
7 It's awful when cars _____ me.	Es ist furchtbar, wenn Autos mich **nass spritzen**.
8 I have to stay in as a _____.	Ich muss als **Strafe** zu Hause bleiben.
9 _____ _____ _____ _____ _____, we all had fun.	**Aus meiner Sicht** hatten wir alle Spaß.

17 True or false?

Sind die Aussagen wahr oder falsch?

	True	False
1 You clear the dishes at the start of a meal.	◯	◯
2 If something is magical, it is very special.	◯	◯
3 Your teacher or your parents could give you a punishment if you behave well.	◯	◯
4 If you throw a stick in a river, it goes downstream.	◯	◯
5 When you are tired, you have lots of energy.	◯	◯
6 A corridor is a small room in a building.	◯	◯
7 When it is cloudy, it is difficult to see the stars.	◯	◯
8 "Steep" sounds the same as "cheap".	◯	◯
9 Chairs, tables, windows and doors are all furniture.	◯	◯
10 "Stupid" is the opposite of "intelligent".	◯	◯
11 Birds have two legs or two wings.	◯	◯
12 Your hero is someone who has done something very good.	◯	◯

3 Unit

A weekend in Liverpool

1 Words and phrases → (pp. 45–47)

1 We _____ the city for a few hours.	Wir **erforschten** die Stadt ein paar Stunden lang.
2 Then we went on a _____ on the river.	Dann machten wir eine **Bootsfahrt** auf dem Fluss.
3 The FIFA World Cup is an _____ competition.	Die FIFA Fußball-Weltmeisterschaft ist ein **internationaler** Wettbewerb.
4 _____ made Liverpool rich.	Die **Sklaverei** hat Liverpool reich gemacht.
5 People bought and sold _____ in the city.	Man hat **Sklaven** in der Stadt gekauft und verkauft.
6 Museums sell souvenirs and _____ like that.	Museen verkaufen Souvenirs und ähnliches **Zeug**.
7 Food first! _____ _____, we can go shopping.	Zuerst Essen! **Danach** können wir einkaufen gehen.
8 Is it _____ to eat five eggs for breakfast?	Ist es **normal**, fünf Eier zum Frühstück zu essen?
9 I wanted to go, but the others _____.	Ich wollte weg, aber die anderen haben **protestiert**.
10 Was there any _____ about the homework?	Gab es wegen der Hausaufgabe **Protest**?
11 I bought a _____ about Liverpool.	Ich habe einen **Reiseführer** für Liverpool gekauft.
12 The book was _____ expensive but very good.	Das Buch war **ziemlich** teuer, aber sehr gut.
13 They look like _____, but _____ you _____ them before you eat them.	Sie sehen aus wie **Bananen**, aber **eigentlich kochst** du sie, bevor du sie isst.

2 Different sounds

Welches Wort hat einen anderen Vokallaut als die anderen drei in der Gruppe? Kreise das Wort ein.

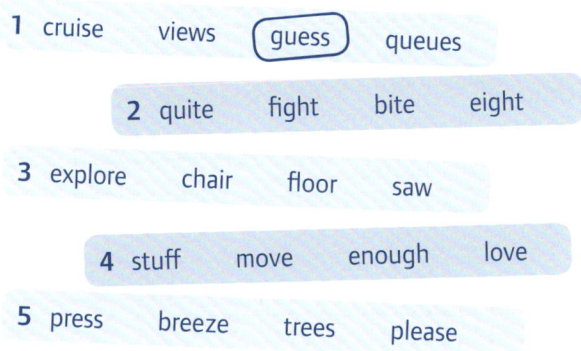

1 cruise   views   (guess)   queues

2 quite   fight   bite   eight

3 explore   chair   floor   saw

4 stuff   move   enough   love

5 press   breeze   trees   please

6 stay   fly   try   die

7 meal   feel   oil   seal

8 good   blood   wood   stood

9 worth   work   worm   worn

10 thief   deep   meant   mean

3 Words and phrases ➜ (pp. 48–49)

> *Wynne was born in Liverpool in 1871.

1 Horace Jones, architect of Tower Bridge isn't very _____ _____: he wasn't even an _____.	Horace Jones, Architekt der Tower Bridge, ist nicht sehr **bekannt**: Er war nicht mal **Ingenieur**.
2 Who is your favourite _____?	Wer ist dein Lieblings**sportler**?
3 My dad isn't a _____: he _____ posters.	Mein Vater ist kein **Soldat**: Er **entwirft** Poster.
4 This is his best _____ this year, I think.	Das ist sein bestes **Design** dieses Jahr, denke ich.
5 Emil Rathenau _____ AEG in 1883.	Emil Rathenau **gründete** AEG 1883.
6 In 1913, A. Wynne* _____ the _____.	1913 **erfand** Arthur Wynne das **Kreuzworträtsel**.
7 I would like to be a _____ of a choir.	Ich würde gerne **Mitglied** eines Chors werden.

4 Definitions

Was wird hier beschrieben?
Trag die Wörter in das Kreuzworträtsel ein.

1 A man or woman who plays e. g. football or tennis.

2 What you do in the kitchen to make a hot meal.

3 Someone who is not free, and who works for no money.

4 A book tourists use with information about places.

5 A person who builds things like bridges.

6 What you do when you think of something new.

7 A person who is part of a team or a club.

8 Someone who wears a uniform and fights.

> *Carl Wilhelm became William and was made a knight by Queen Victoria.

5 Correct the mistakes

Verbessere einen Fehler in jedem Satz und schreibe das Wort richtig auf.

1 We learned a lot about sklavery in the museum. _____

2 The Tower of London is a well-know attraction. _____

3 He said he knew the answer, but actual he was wrong. _____

4 This club is very old. They found it a hundred years ago. _____

5 Sir William Siemens was a famous ingineer who lived in England.* _____

Lösungen

1 Personal details A–Z

1 aunt   **2** boarding school   **3** countries   **4** divorced
5 English   **6** funny   **7** girl   **8** Happy   **9** in   **10** kid
11 live   **12** mum   **13** names   **14** old   **15** partner
16 road   **17** single   **18** twins   **19** uncle   **20** woman
21 young

Fehlende Buchstaben: J; Q; V; X; Z

2 Word fields

Colours: brown; dark; green; pink; purple; yellow
Shapes and sizes: circle; large; little; long; short; tall
Quantities: double; group; half; mile; second; unit
Materials: paper; plastic; rock; rubber; silky; stone

3 Scrambled words

1 alone   **2** across   **3** behind   **4** between   **5** far
6 inside   **7** narrow   **8** past   **9** under   **10** further

4 People and things

1 H   **2** E   **3** G   **4** L   **5** N   **6** A   **7** D   **8** B   **9** C
10 O   **11** F   **12** K   **13** I   **14** M

5 Word fields

1 ~~tractor~~ → farmer   **2** ~~text~~ → recorder
3 ~~farmer~~ → tractor   **4** ~~butterfly~~ → text
5 ~~recorder~~ → hay   **6** ~~hay~~ → butterfly

Mögliche Überschriften:
1 Jobs   **2** Music   **3** Transport   **4** Communication
5 Nature   **6** Animals

6 Irregular verbs

1 blew   **2** drew; drawn   **3** fought   **4** knew; known
5 made   **6** meet   **7** ran   **8** took   **9** thought
10 understood

7 True or false

1 True   **2** False   **3** False   **4** False   **5** True   **6** False
7 True   **8** False   **9** True   **10** True

8 Crossword

Crossword solution:

- 1 down: MILK
- 2 across: CLOCK
- 3 down: CHAIR
- 4 down: DANCE
- 5 across: BOX
- 5 down: BRIDGE
- 6 across: G
- 7 across: CHAMPION
- 8 across: SIGN
- 9 down: NECK
- 10 down: BAG
- 11 across: ARM
- 11 down: FARMER
- 12 across: DOG
- 12 down: DEEN
- 13 down: TOWEL
- 14 across: CA
- 15 down: TEETH
- 16 across: NOSE
- 17 across: BOAT
- 17 down: BELL
- 18 down: FINGER
- 19 across: CHURC
- 20 down: HAIR
- 21 down: FEE
- 22 across: T
- 23 across: GUITAR
- 22 down: TICKE
- 24 down: LEG
- 25 across: PRIZE
- 26 across: DOCTOR
- 26 down: DES
- 27 down: EGG
- 28 down: HEAR
- 29 down: BIRD
- 30 across: TONGUE
- 31 down: BOW
- 32 across: KNIFE
- 33 across: FOOTBALL

9 Wrong weather!

1 temperature   2 lightning   3 rainy   4 thunder
5 cooler   6 weather   7 flash   8 sunny   9 mist
10 snow

10 Join the sentences

1 E   2 F   3 H   4 G   5 C   6 A   7 B   8 D

11 The fourth word

1 listener   2 climb   3 song   4 swimmer   5 flower
6 turn off   7 paw   8 queen   9 never   10 ours
11 teeth   12 invite

12 Compound nouns

appointment; background; classmate; disappear;
grandparents; highlight; neighbour; sharpener;
timetable

Unit 1

1 Words and phrases

1 best; thing; about; huge   2 as soon as   3 cathedral
4 palace   5 Welsh   6 replied; to   7 western; Europe
8 I see   9 lift   10 amazing   11 How   12 post

2 Q & A

1 e   2 f   3 a   4 b   5 g   6 c   7 h   8 d

3 Words and phrases

1 Carnival   2 test   3 into   4 enjoy   5 By the way
6 south   7 darkness   8 clue   9 skyline   10 false
11 go; together   12 on; Tube   13 underground
14 stay; at   15 timetable; gallery   16 restaurant

4 What are they describing?

1 timetable   2 restaurant   3 darkness   4 gallery
5 post   6 the Tube   7 false   8 skyline

5 Words and phrases

1 stress   2 stress marks   3 small talk   4 culture
5 expect   6 attraction   7 natural history   8 entry
9 the UK   10 reserve   11 in fact   12 fact
13 steps   14 chance

6 Missing words

1 stress; season; syllable   2 ticket; entry; free
3 call; reserve; evening   4 country; Europe; culture
5 thing; time; history   6 sport; enjoy; way
7 big; good; small   8 well; felt; fact

7 Words and phrases

1 figures   2 less; than   3 tortoise
4 on top of each other   5 parliament   6 at one time
7 Christmas   8 ticket office   9 detail
10 adult   11 family; of; ten   12 during   13 guard
14 ravens; blood   15 is; home; to; Jewels

8 The fourth word

1 south   2 true   3 cathedral   4 red   5 adults
6 less   7 bird   8 dark/darkness

9 Words and phrases

1 instead of   2 exact   3 linking; words   4 link
5 queue   6 worth   7 were; roaring   8 crowded

10 Missing words

1 Christmas   2 into   3 figures   4 steps   5 one
6 famous   7 parliament   8 interesting   9 ravens
10 guard   11 surprised   12 biscuits
13 blood   14 jewels   15 during   16 birthday
17 office   18 instead of

11 Words and phrases

1 feedback   2 improve   3 react to
4 content   5 connect   6 pointed; out; to; me
7 lines   8 northbound; southbound
9 change

12 Wrong!

1 useful; feedback   2 example; connect
3 some; spelling   4 English; improving
5 southbound; northbound   6 gallery; queue
7 attractions; together   8 exact; worth

13 Words and phrases

1 was; slow   2 isn't; working   3 head; for
4 announcement   5 message   6 platform   7 is; on
8 No way   9 for   10 since   11 and; anyway
12 try

14 Join the parts

1 tortoise   2 announcement   3 message   4 anyway
5 platform   6 details   7 content   8 expect

15 Words and phrases

1 remote; control   2 turn; up   3 each other   4 pub
5 for; a; while   6 tap   7 Off; you; go; now   8 towards
9 tense   10 went; on   11 situation

16 Scrambled story

1 A   2 E   3 C   4 H   5 D   6 G   7 F   8 B

17 Words and phrases

1 route   2 speed   3 It's; a; pity   4 Hold; on; to
5 scanned; for   6 fill   7 pavement

18 Missing words

1 –/the   2 –/as   3 of/–   4 –/you   5 –/of
6 –/do   7 a/–   8 on/–   9 a/–   10 out/–

19 Words and phrases

1 available   2 all; around   3 whistle   4 blew; whistle
5 panicked   6 exactly   7 bent; down; rope
8 wings; rainbow   9 dizzy   10 hips; you   11 rhythm
12 loudspeaker; scared   13 Do; mind; rest
14 no; sign; of   15 under; my; breath

20 True or false?

1 False   2 True   3 False   4 True   5 True   6 False
7 True   8 False

Unit 2

1 Words and phrases

1 empty   2 Scientists; study   3 workshop; carpenter
4 furniture; is   5 oil; piece; of   6 hammer
7 coming; over   8 make; fun; of   9 give; up
10 tonight

2 Match the parts

1 e   2 d   3 f   4 a   5 g   6 b   7 c   8 h

3 Words and phrases

1 architect   2 astronaut   3 hairdresser   4 musician
5 painter   6 natural; world   7 headword
8 part of speech   9 translation   10 coal; underground
11 grounded   12 official; official   13 police; are

4 Come and look

1 looking into   2 come up with   3 look it up
4 come over   5 come across   6 come down with
7 looked up   8 looking forward to   9 look around
10 look after

5 Words and phrases

1 national   2 altogether   3 hostel   4 wonder
5 pretend   6 Me neither   7 went; by   8 stupid
9 downstream   10 edge   11 reach   12 stick; grabbed

6 Which verb?

1 go   2 make   3 coming   4 wonder   5 looking
6 reach   7 come   8 give

7 Words and phrases

1 steep   2 sang; along   3 joined; in   4 Before; long
5 told; not; to   6 warning   7 movie   8 head; teacher
9 allow

8 So much stress

Stress on the first syllable:
warning; stupid; empty
Stress on the second syllable:
tonight; enough; allow

9 Missing letters

1 altogether   2 neither   3 underground   4 edge
5 oil   6 scientist

10 Words and phrases

1 topic; sentence   2 connected   3 3.5; point
4 climb; summit   5 1,000; managed   6 continued
7 downhill   8 energy   9 a; total; of   10 bar; hero
11 revised   12 organized; added

11 Make pairs

turn off the TV; reply to an email;
look forward to the holidays; head for the city centre;
scan the crowd; blow the whistle;
come over to my house; look for my house keys;
revise my work; make up a story

12 Words and phrases

1 difficult   2 carrot   3 press   4 finally
5 was; able; meal   6 keep; making   7 silently; corridor
8 stars; magical   9 lie; down   10 busy
11 clear   12 breeze   13 have; a; look; at   14 sat; up
15 wooden   16 wide; figure

13 Word groups

Things in a city:
cathedral; gallery; pavement; pub; underground
The natural world:
breeze; coal; rainbow; star; summit
The world of work:
director; head teacher; official; police; scientist
Wörter, die nicht passen:
dizzy; spelling

14 Words and phrases

1 notes   2 such; a; so   3 did; make; up   4 argue
5 bite   6 director   7 office

15 Almost the same

1 e   2 d   3 k   4 i   5 h   6 a   7 l   8 b   9 j
10 f   11 g   12 c

16 Words and phrases

1 how; to   2 what; to   3 where; to   4 who; to
5 behave   6 mop; mop   7 splash   8 punishment
9 From; my; point ; of; view

17 True or false?

1 False   2 True   3 False   4 True   5 False
6 False   7 True   8 True   9 False   10 True
11 False   12 True

Unit 3

1 Words and phrases

1 explored   2 cruise   3 international   4 Slavery
5 slaves   6 stuff   7 After; that   8 normal
9 protested   10 protest   11 guidebook   12 quite
13 bananas; actually; cook

2 Different sounds

1 guess   2 eight   3 chair   4 move   5 press
6 stay   7 oil   8 blood   9 worn

3 Words and phrases

1 well; known; engineer   2 sportsperson
3 soldier; designs   4 design   5 founded
6 invented; crossword   7 member

4 Definitions

The crossword grid contains:
- 1 Down: SPORTSPERSON
- 2 Across: COOK
- 3 Down: SLAVE
- 4 Down: GUIDEBOOK
- 5 Down: ENGINEER
- 6 Across: INVENT
- 7 Across: MEMBER
- 8 Across: SOLDIER

5 Correct the mistakes

1 slavery   2 well-known   3 actually   4 founded
5 engineer

6 Words and phrases

1 introduction   2 body   3 conclusion   4 several
5 opinion   6 ends   7 schedule   8 is; having; a; day; off
9 earn   10 experience   11 As; was; born   12 grew; up
13 modern

7 True or false?

1 True   2 True   3 False   4 False   5 True   6 True
7 False   8 False

8 Words and phrases

1 success   2 perform   3 popular; with
4 monument; to   5 two-hour   6 Remember
7 remember   8 in; an; way   9 in; some; ways   10 if

9 Match the sentences

1 D   2 G   3 A   4 H   5 I   6 C   7 F   8 B
9 J   10 E

10 Words and phrases

1 led   2 leader; trade   3 mask; horns   4 people
5 clay   6 shapes   7 pot; carry   8 bare   9 respect
10 ancestors   11 captives; plantations
12 cruel; survive   13 conditions   14 triangle

11 More about the slave trade

1 A   2 D   3 H   4 B   5 F   6 J   7 G   8 I   9 C
10 E   11 K

12 Words and phrases

1 room   2 material   3 covered   4 contest
5 net; goal   6 airport   7 community   8 mosque
9 score; half-time   10 what; was; final; score
11 sunshine

13 Odd one out

1 stadium   2 beach   3 road   4 theatre   5 friends

14 Match the parts

1 E   2 F   3 A   4 B   5 D   6 C

15 Words and phrases

1 referee   2 goalkeeper   3 order; structure
4 equipment   5 stadium   6 pitch   7 manager; scarf
8 free; kick   9 bully   10 solve   11 slow; motion

16 Broken words

1 crossword   2 equipment   3 monument   4 referee
5 manager   6 community   7 stadium   8 protest
9 engineer   10 several

17 Words and phrases

1 no   2 canal   3 is; shining; shone   4 laughter
5 surface   6 seem   7 burn   8 drowned   9 Nowhere
10 out; of; nowhere   11 dive; in

18 Word partners

loudspeaker; free kick; slow motion; bare feet;
final score; local shops; cruel person; popular music;
busy schedule; natural history

19 Words and phrases

1 marry   2 career; sailor   3 body   4 local   5 spread
6 funeral   7 take; place   8 name

20 The right words

1 as; grew up   2 place; stadium   3 career; sailor
4 happy; laughter   5 wore; carried   6 material; shape
7 drowned; surface   8 nowhere; look
9 opinion; modern   10 hero; invented

Unit 4

1 Words and phrases

1 impression   2 brochure; practical   3 northern
4 coffee   5 giant   6 might   7 as well   8 columns
9 rise; up; nearly   10 formed   11 proud of
12 challenge   13 challenged   14 left; Shall
15 curious   16 advert; polite   17 impolite

2 Match the sentences

1 E   2 G   3 D   4 A   5 B   6 C   7 F

3 Missing verbs

1 takes 2 drive 3 might 4 be 5 looks 6 are
7 rise 8 create 9 form 10 goes

4 More missing verbs

1 says 2 made 3 challenged 4 agreed 5 built
6 walk 7 swim 8 met 9 fought 10 won

5 Words and phrases

Countries which are not in the EU but use the euro:
Andorra, Monaco, San Marino and Vatican City.

1 border 2 change 3 currency; EU; euro 4 cents
5 ID card 6 Nations 7 passports 8 peace; War
9 police station 10 population 11 President; republic
12 States 13 visa 14 pet; stolen 15 bank

6 Define the words

1 republic (or country, *but think of the Queen*)
2 countries 3 number; people
4 fight 5 animal; family 6 border 7 money
8 euro (or dollar)

7 Words and phrases

1 coordinator 2 layout 3 editor 4 research
5 result 6 suggest 7 discussion 8 decision

8 -er or -or?

1 actor; border 2 doctor; director 3 editor; visitors
4 coordinator; leader 5 better; ancestors
6 sailor; soldier

9 Wrong!

1 passports 2 research 3 decision 4 peace
5 republic

10 Words and phrases

1 Angels; heaven 2 service 3 Check out 4 was like
5 motorbike 6 suit 7 smoke; pipe 8 like 9 hell
10 by 11 have a shower 12 electronic 13 Atlantic
14 beginning 15 in the beginning 16 guest
17 facial expression 18 interaction

11 Word partners

change money; check something out;
explore a new place; have a shower; keep notes;
lie down; rise up; smoke a pipe; take place;
wear a suit

12 Words and phrases

1 arrival 2 weird 3 ride 4 alive 5 argument
6 miss 7 round here 8 stare 9 care about
10 don't care 11 am starving 12 unpack 13 God
14 dislike

13 Broken words

1 unpacked 2 starving 3 dislike 4 weird
5 argument 6 arrival 7 electronic 8 result
9 facial 10 service

14 Words and phrases

1 bang 2 regional accent 3 Standard
4 boyfriend; girlfriend 5 welcome to 6 passes
7 next 8 Easter 9 junction 10 pedestrian

15 The fourth word

1 boyfriend 2 hell 3 pedestrians 4 pounds
5 eyes 6 shower

16 Join the parts

1 d 2 e 3 a 4 b 5 c

17 Words and phrases

1 walk 2 kick 3 raced 4 traffic lights
5 traffic 6 turn 7 van 8 spin around 9 park
10 immediately 11 siren 12 Are; gone

18 Scrambled story

1 A 2 G 3 F 4 B 5 I 6 D 7 H 8 J
9 C 10 E

19 Words and phrases

1 None of 2 a couple of 3 folk 4 line
5 What's up 6 trail 7 sighed 8 now that
9 slippery 10 ditch

20 The right words

1 a 2 up 3 that 4 of 5 by 6 days 7 alive
8 like 9 left 10 as

21 Words and phrases

1 in the old days   2 gravestone   3 buried
4 famine disease   5 emigrated   6 government
7 exports   8 stream   9 ash   10 glad; death
11 especially   12 thought

22 True or false?

1 True   2 False   3 False   4 True   5 True
6 False   7 True   8 False   9 True   10 False
11 False   12 True

Unit 5

1 Words and phrases

1 extraordinary   2 is promoting   3 bagpipes
4 Look out   5 competing in   6 sheepdog; trials
7 Highlands   8 on board; yacht   9 wee
10 isle   11 identify; dolphins   12 social media
13 unusual   14 usually

Heligoland: That was the name of the island between
1807 and 1890, when it was a British colony.

2 Friends

calm sea; expensive yacht; green light; late arrival;
loud noise; regional accent; Scottish Highlands;
slippery ground; social media

3 Match the parts

1 E   2 D   3 H   4 I   5 B   6 J   7 C   8 F
9 A   10 G

4 The right pair

1 about; to   2 for; in   3 With; on   4 on; of
5 about; in   6 in; for   7 to; by   8 of; to   9 on; out
10 after; at

What's wrong? The dorsal fins are all the same!

5 Words and phrases

1 volunteer   2 sightings   3 put; hand up
4 photograph; pollution   5 spend time
6 spent; money   7 protect   8 teach   9 dorsal fin

6 Quiz questions

1 volunteer   2 isle   3 dorsal fin   4 photograph
5 put your hand up   6 pollution   7 spend
8 bagpipes

7 The right words

1 sightings; of   2 spent; sights   3 taught; when
4 teach; photograph

8 Words and phrases

1 record   2 location   3 monitor   4 movement
5 rough   6 calm; seasick   7 keep   8 kept   9 relax
10 escape   11 escape   12 split screen

9 Match the sentences

1 F   2 G   3 I   4 A   5 B   6 H   7 D   8 J
9 C   10 E

10 Words and phrases

1 cue   2 fault   3 backstage   4 rehearsal
5 no one else   6 concentrate   7 picks on
8 am tired of   9 position

11 True or false?

1 True   2 True   3 False   4 False   5 False
6 True   7 False

12 The fourth word

1 impolite   2 peace   3 movement   4 ride   5 kick
6 death

13 Words and phrases

1 tough   2 trod on; toes   3 gave a hard time
4 calm down   5 description   6 direct
7 whenever   8 Whatever   9 platforms   10 comedian
11 entertainment   12 interests

14 So much stress

First syllabus stress ['---]:
concentrate; emigrate; government; motorbike;
photograph; president; slippery
Second syllable stress [-'--]:
Atlantic; beginning; continue; location; pollution;
rehearsal; whenever
Third syllable stress [--'-]:
disappear; engineer; impolite; indirect; interrupt;
referee; volunteer

15 Words and phrases

1 handout   **2** transparency   **3** lynx   **4** lynxes; habitat
5 coat   **6** predator   **7** mammal   **8** territory
9 element   **10** necessary

16 Broken words

1 handout   **2** habitat   **3** predators   **4** coat
5 necessary   **6** territory   **7** protect   **8** Lynxes
9 mammals   **10** transparency

17 Words and phrases

1 Missing   **2** heather   **3** below   **4** above   **5** tension
6 whistle   **7** in horror   **8** noise   **9** reached over
10 dry   **11** beat   **12** read; mind   **13** Shepherds

18 Rhymes

1 below; go   **2** dry; high   **3** tough; stuff   **4** noise; boys
5 lynx; thinks   **6** made; afraid   **7** taught; thought
8 cue; through   **9** compete; beat   **10** calm; farm

19 Words and phrases

1 jealous   **2** hate   **3** burst into tears   **4** gently
5 awake; knocked   **6** memorial   **7** in second place

20 Word fields

Sea: Atlantic; dolphin; lifejacket; on board; yacht
Place: border; habitat; local; northern; regional
Feelings: glad; hate; horror; jealous; miss
Work: career; editor; office; shepherd; suit
Noise: bang; knock; sigh; siren; whistle
Social media: computer; platform; screen; send; text

21 Scrambled story

1 A   **2** I   **3** E   **4** B   **5** G   **6** J   **7** F   **8** L   **9** C
10 M   **11** D   **12** H   **13** K

22 Missing words

1 starving; round   **2** brochure; impression
3 suggested; shower   **4** knocked; awake
5 burst; trod   **6** hard; walk   **7** name; rainbow
8 sign; gone   **9** argument; pretending
10 practical; translation

23 Crossword

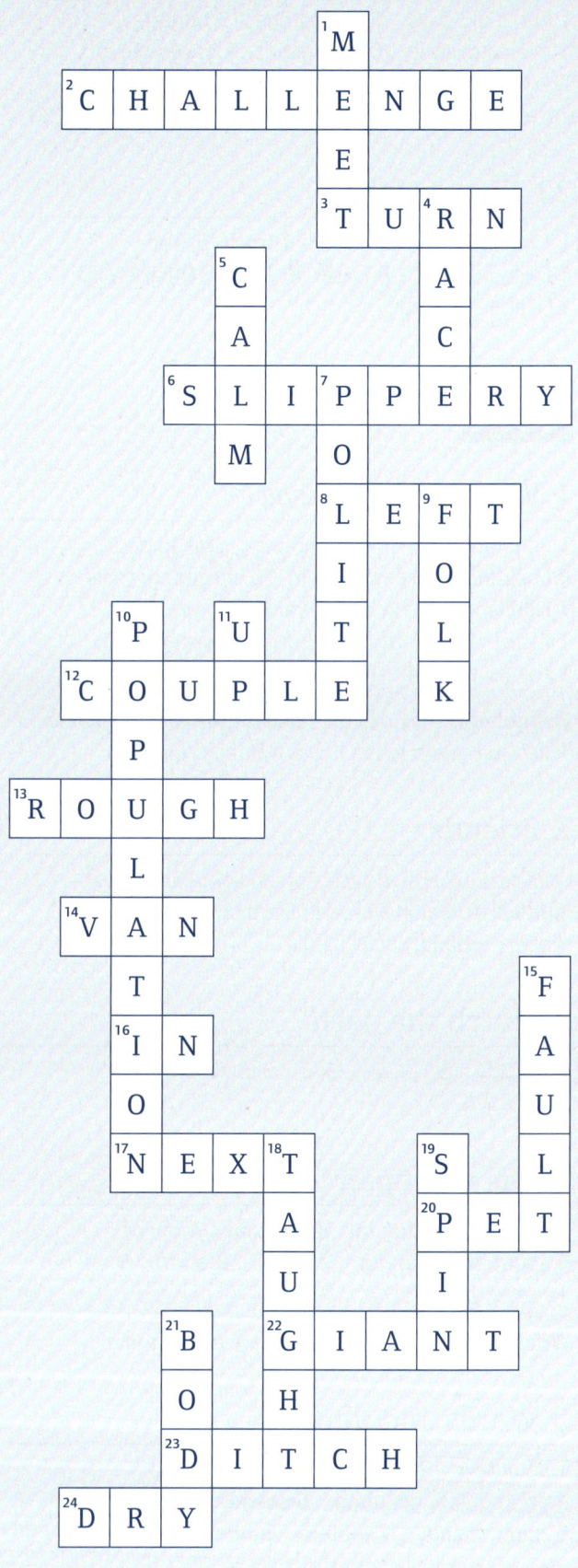

6 Words and phrases ➜ (p. 51)

1 The _____ is the first part of a text.	Der erste Teil eines Textes ist die **Einleitung**.
2 Then comes the _____.	Dann folgt der **Hauptteil**.
3 At the end is the _____.	Am Ende ist der **Schluss**.
4 I've seen the film _____ times.	Ich habe den Film **mehrere** Male gesehen.
5 In my _____ it's the best film of the year.	**Meiner Meinung nach** ist er der beste Film des Jahres.
6 It _____ with a really good song.	Er **endet** mit einem wirklich guten Lied.
7 We have a very full _____ this week.	Wir haben ein sehr volles **Programm** diese Woche.
8 Mum ___ _____ __ ____ _____ next week.	Mama **hat** nächste Woche **einen Tag frei**.
9 Most people work hard to _____ money.	Die meisten arbeiten schwer, um Geld zu **verdienen**.
10 At least that's the _____ of my parents.	Das ist zumindest die **Erfahrung** meiner Eltern.
11 ____ you know, Mum _____ _____ in Hamburg.	**Wie** du weißt: Mutti **ist** in Hamburg **geboren**.
12 But she _____ _____ in Templin.	Aber sie **ist** in Templin **aufgewachsen**.
13 When did _____ art begin?	Wann hat die **Moderne** Kunst begonnen?

7 True or false?

Sind die Aussagen wahr oder falsch?

True   False

1 When people protest, they want to change something.

2 Facts are different from opinions.

3 People have days off every Monday.

4 "Several" means the same as "once or twice".

5 Bananas are often yellow or green, but not red.

6 Introductions come before conclusions.

7 Doing crosswords is a sport.

8 Finding money and earning money are the same.

8 Words and phrases → *(p. 51)*

It's in Ulaanbaatar and was opened in 2008.

1 What in your opinion is the key to _____?	Was ist deiner Meinung nach der Schlüssel zum **Erfolg**?
2 I get nervous when I _____ on stage.	Ich bin aufgeregt, wenn ich auf der Bühne **auftrete**.
3 The Beatles are _____ _____ many people.	Die Beatles sind **bei** vielen Leuten **beliebt**.
4 Mongolia* has a _____ _____ the Beatles.	In der Mongolei steht ein **Denkmal für** die Beatles.
5 The _____ journey was very nice.	Die **zweistündige** Fahrt war sehr schön.
6 _____ to buy some milk tomorrow.	**Denk daran**, morgen Milch zu kaufen.
7 Dad can never _____ Mum's birthday.	Papa kann **sich** nie Mamas Geburtstag **merken**.
8 You eat pizza ____ ____ interesting _____!	Du isst Pizza **auf eine** interessante **Art und Weise**!
9 England and Wales are similar ____ _____ _____.	England und Wales sind **in mancher Hinsicht** ähnlich.
10 Do you know ____ the station is near here?	Weißt du, **ob** der Bahnhof hier in der Nähe ist?

...interesting!

9 Match the sentences

Verbinde die Sätze, die eine ähnliche Bedeutung haben.

1 I had an interesting experience.	**A** I've forgotten. Sorry.
2 I don't know if that's right.	**B** I've got a lot of things to do.
3 I'm afraid I can't remember.	**C** We all had a great time.
4 They are quite popular.	**D** You'll never guess what happened.
5 The conclusion isn't very good.	**E** There are people from many countries.
6 The party was a big success.	**F** I really like the way they play.
7 I think their music is great.	**G** I'm not very sure about that, actually.
8 Today's schedule is really busy.	**H** A lot of people like them.
9 It's just a five-minute walk.	**I** The way it ends could be better.
10 It's a very international group.	**J** It's not very far from here.

10 Words and phrases ➜ *(pp. 54–55)*

1 Our group was _____ through the rooms.	Unsere Gruppe wurde durch die Räume **geführt**.
2 The _____ told us about the slave _____.	Der **Leiter** hat uns vom Sklaven**handel** erzählt.
3 There was a _____ with _____ like an animal.	Es gab eine **Maske** mit **Hörnern** wie bei einem Tier.
4 I learned about the history of the Igbo _____.	Ich lernte etwas über die Geschichte des Igbo-**Volks**.
5 They use _____ to make drums.	Sie verwenden **Lehm**, um Trommel zu bauen.
6 The drums are different _____.	Die Trommeln haben verschiedene **Formen**.
7 One looked like a _____ to _____ water in.	Eine sah aus wie ein **Topf** zum Wasser**tragen**.
8 I like to run on wet grass in _____ feet.	Ich laufe gerne auf nassem Rasen mit **nackten** Füssen.
9 Be friendly and show _____ to others.	Sei freundlich und zeig anderen gegenüber **Respekt**.
10 It's good to learn about our _____.	Es ist gut, etwas über unsere **Vorfahren** zu lernen.
11 African _____ lived on _____.	Afrikanische **Gefangene** lebten auf **Plantagen**.
12 Life was _____: many did not _____ long.	Das Leben war **grausam**: Viele **überlebten** nicht lange.
13 Their _____ were terrible.	Ihre **Bedingungen** waren furchtbar.
14 Our teacher told us about the trade _____.	Unser Lehrer erzählte uns vom Handels**dreieck**.

11 More about the slave trade

Verbinde die Satzteile so, dass sie einen zusammenhängenden Text ergeben.

A We learn about the slave trade in history lessons or when we visit

E holidays. The people who owned them expected them to continue until

F like animals to work on plantations and farms. They lived in terrible

B homes in Africa to new countries. There they were bought and sold

G and the children did not go to school. One of the most terrible things

C and every year was the same. There was no free time, and they had no

H millions of men, women and children who were taken from their

D museums. These tell us some of the terrible facts about slavery, about the

I about life as a slave was that they had no future. Every day, every month

J conditions and had no freedom. They earned no money for their work,

K they died.

Answer: ⒜ ◯ ◯ ◯ ◯ ◯ ◯ ◯ ◯ Ⓚ

12 Words and phrases → *(pp. 54–57)*

1 There is not enough _____ to build a house here.	Hier gibt es nicht genug **Platz**, um ein Haus zu bauen.
2 What _____ is your shirt?	Aus welchem **Stoff** ist dein Hemd?
3 The roof was _____ with grass.	Das Dach war mit Gras **bedeckt**.
4 We have a singing _____ every year.	Wir haben jedes Jahr einen Gesangs**wettbewerb**.
5 We need a new _____ for the _____.	Wir brauchen ein neues **Netz** für das **Tor**.
6 The school is not far from the _____.	Die Schule ist nicht weit vom **Flughafen**.
7 Liverpool has a big Chinese _____.	Liverpool hat eine große chinesische **Gemeinde**.
8 The city also has the oldest _____ in England.*	Die Stadt hat auch die älteste **Moschee** Englands.
9 The _____ at _____ was 5:0.	Der **Spielstand** zur **Halbzeit** war 5:0.
10 And _____ _____ the _____ _____?	Und **wie stand es** am **Ende**?
11 Everyone enjoyed the _____ in the park.	Alle genossen den **Sonnenschein** im Park.

*The Liverpool Muslim Institute was opened in 1887.

13 Odd one out

Welches Wort in jeder Gruppe passt nicht zu den anderen? Schreibe es rechts auf.

1 church mosque cathedral stadium _____

2 sunshine beach rain storm _____

3 river sea road canal _____

4 theatre contest competition match _____

5 ancestors friends parents family _____

14 Match the parts

Verbinde die Fragen links mit den Sätzen rechts. Bilde Dialoge.

1 Did you have a fantastic weekend?

2 Is this your first time in Liverpool?

3 Can I sit next to you?

4 Is the mask made of wood?

5 Do you know the score?

6 Do you know the name of that shape?

A No, sorry, there's no room.

B No, clay.

C No. Not sure. Is it a triangle?

D No, sorry, I don't.

E No, it was normal.

F No, I grew up here.

15 Words and phrases ➜ *(pp. 58–59)*

1 The _____ blew his whistle. The game was over.	Der **Schiedsrichter** pfiff. Das Spiel war vorbei.
2 The _____ was angry with his team.	Der **Torwart** war wütend auf seine Mannschaft.
3 _____ your ideas to _____ your text.	**Ordne** deine Ideen, um deinen Text zu **gliedern**.
4 Before the game, she checked the _____.	Vor dem Spiel prüfte sie die **Ausrüstung**.
5 My favourite _____ is in a Berlin forest.	Mein Lieblings**stadion** steht in einem Berliner Wald.
6 We had a great view of the _____.	Wir hatten einen guten Ausblick auf das **Spielfeld**.
7 Our _____ wore red trainers and a _____.	Unser **Trainer** trug rote Turnschuhe und einen **Schal**.
8 I scored from a _____ _____.	Ich erzielte einen Treffer durch einen **Freistoß**.
9 If someone is a _____, tell Dad.	Wenn jemand ein **Tyrann** ist, sag Papa Bescheid.
10 I had a problem, but was able to _____ it.	Ich hatte ein Problem, konnte es aber **lösen**.
11 They show the goals in _____ _____ on TV.	Im Fernsehen werden die Tore in **Zeitlupe** gezeigt.

16 Broken words

Verbinde die Wortteile und vervollständige die Sätze mit den Wörtern.

1 Are you reading the paper? – No, I'm doing the _____.

2 You need the right _____ to play sports.

3 I took a photo of the _____.

4 The match ended when the _____ blew his whistle.

5 The _____ of the team told them how to play.

6 Is there a big foreign _____ where you live?

7 We live right next to the football _____.

8 We heard the noise of the _____ in the city centre.

9 My dad's an _____. He designs bridges and stuff.

10 I've been to London _____ times.

sev · cross · ref · test · u · mon · pro · man · e · ment · a · ee · com · word · mun · quip · i · ity · stad · gin · en · um · ger · eer · er · al · ment · er

17 Words and phrases ➡ *(p. 60)*

1 It was hot in June, and it was _____ different in July.	Es war heiß im Juni, und im Juli **nicht** anders.
2 That isn't a river. It's a _____!	Das ist kein Fluss. Es ist ein **Kanal**!
3 The sun ____ _____. It _____ yesterday too.	Die Sonne **scheint** jetzt. Sie **schien** auch gestern.
4 I can hear _____ from the classroom.	Ich kann aus dem Klassenzimmer **Gelächter** hören.
5 There are bottles on the _____ of the water.	Da sind Flaschen auf der **Oberfläche** des Wassers.
6 We all _____ to be ready now.	Wir **scheinen** alle jetzt fertig zu sein.
7 Don't drink the soup yet. You'll _____ yourself.	Iss die Suppe noch nicht. Du wirst dich **verbrennen**.
8 A woman nearly _____ in the river today.	Eine Frau **ist** heute im Fluss fast **ertrunken**.
9 _____ is as nice as home.	**Nirgendwo** ist es so schön wie zu Hause.
10 A man came _____ ____ _____ and saw her.	Ein Mann kam **aus dem Nichts** und sah sie.
11 Please _____ ____ and get my ball.	**Spring** bitte **hinein** und hol meinen Ball.

18 Word partners

Verbinde die Teile so, dass sie sinnvolle Paare bilden.
(Auf einer Kopie kannst du die Teile ausschneiden. Wenn alles richtig ist, erhältst du eine geometrische Figur.)

loud, kick, feet, person, final, slow, cruel, speaker, natural, popular, motion, music, local, free, score, shops, history, bare, busy, schedule

19 Words and phrases → (p. 61)

1 Suddenly he asked, "Will you _____ me?"	Plötzlich hat er gefragt: „Willst du mich **heiraten**?".
2 Dad's _____ as a _____ began in 1977.	Seine **Karriere** als **Matrose** begann 1977.
3 They found the _____ of the man who drowned.	Sie haben die **Leiche** des Ertrunkenen gefunden.
4 You can buy many things from _____ shops.	Du kannst viele Sachen von Läden **am Ort** kaufen.
5 The sad news _____ quickly.	Die traurigen Nachrichten **verbreiteten** sich schnell.
6 Hundreds will go to his _____.	Hunderte werden zu seiner **Trauerfeier** kommen.
7 It will _____ _____ on Monday.	Sie wird am Montag **stattfinden**.
8 Can you _____ five English football clubs?	Kannst du fünf englische Fußballvereine **nennen**?

20 The right words

Kreise die richtigen Wörter ein, um die Sätze zu vervollständigen.

1 ⟨As⟩ • **So** you know, Lennon **born** • **grew** up in Liverpool.

2 Concerts often take **place** • **state** in this football **pitch** • **stadium** .

3 He had a **career** • **work** as a **soldier** • **sailor** , and lived and worked on the sea.

4 Everyone was **sad** • **happy** . You could hear lots of **laugh** • **laughter** .

5 She **carried** • **wore** a hat on her head and **carried** • **wore** a pot in her hands.

6 I like the **material** • **stuff** of this chair. It is a nice **shape** • **way** too.

7 I nearly **drowned** • **hurt** in the lake. I couldn't get to the **top** • **surface** .

8 He came out of **somewhere** • **nowhere** to have a **look** • **looking** at the match.

9 In my **meaning** • **opinion** , **modern** • **now** music is the best.

10 Who's my **well-known** • **hero** ? The person who **founded** • **invented** holidays!

My trip to Ireland

1 Words and phrases ➜ (pp. 64–66)

1 How was your first _____ of Ireland?	Wie war dein erster **Eindruck** von Irland?
2 This _____ has some _____ tips.	Diese **Broschüre** hat einige **praktische** Tipps.
3 We visited the _____ coast.	Wir haben die **Nord**küste besucht.
4 Would you like a _____?	Möchtest du einen **Kaffee**?
5 He's not just tall: he's a _____!	Er ist nicht nur groß: Er ist ein **Riese**!
6 I _____ be happy if I was richer.	Ich **könnte** glücklich sein, wenn ich reicher wäre.
7 I might ____ ____ go. Nothing's happening.	Ich könnte **ebenso gut** gehen. Nichts passiert hier.
8 We saw a building with tall _____.	Wir sahen ein Gebäude mit großen **Säulen**.
9 – Yes, they _____ ____ _____ 10 metres.	– Ja, sie **ragen fast** 10 Meter **empor**.
10 We _____ a queue and waited.	Wir **bildeten** eine Schlange und warteten.
11 I'm very _____ ____ you for your work.	Ich bin sehr **stolz auf** dich wegen deiner Arbeit.
12 I know it was a _____.	Ich weiß, es war eine **Herausforderung**.
13 – Yes, the problem really _____ me.	– Ja, das Problem **hat** mich wirklich **herausgefordert**.
14 There's nothing _____ to eat. _____ I order pizza?	Es ist nichts zu essen **übrig**. **Soll** ich Pizza bestellen?
15 Because I'm _____, I always want to know why.	Weil ich **neugierig** bin, will ich immer wissen, warum.
16 I read an _____ and sent a _____ email.	Ich las eine **Anzeige** und schrieb eine **höfliche** E-Mail.
17 But their reply was really _____.	Aber die Antwort war wirklich **unhöflich**.

2 Match the sentences

Verbinde die Sätze, die eine ähnliche Bedeutung haben.

1 He's curious about everything.

2 What he said to us wasn't very nice.

3 It wasn't easy for him to do.

4 His dad thinks he is brilliant.

5 He's very tall, isn't he?

6 He said what he thought about it.

7 He's finished it all.

A He's really proud of him.

B He's a giant – well, nearly!

C He told me his impressions.

D It was a challenge for him.

E He asks a lot of questions.

F There's nothing left.

G He was very impolite to us.

3 Missing verbs

Schreib die Verben aus den Feldern in die richtige Lücke.

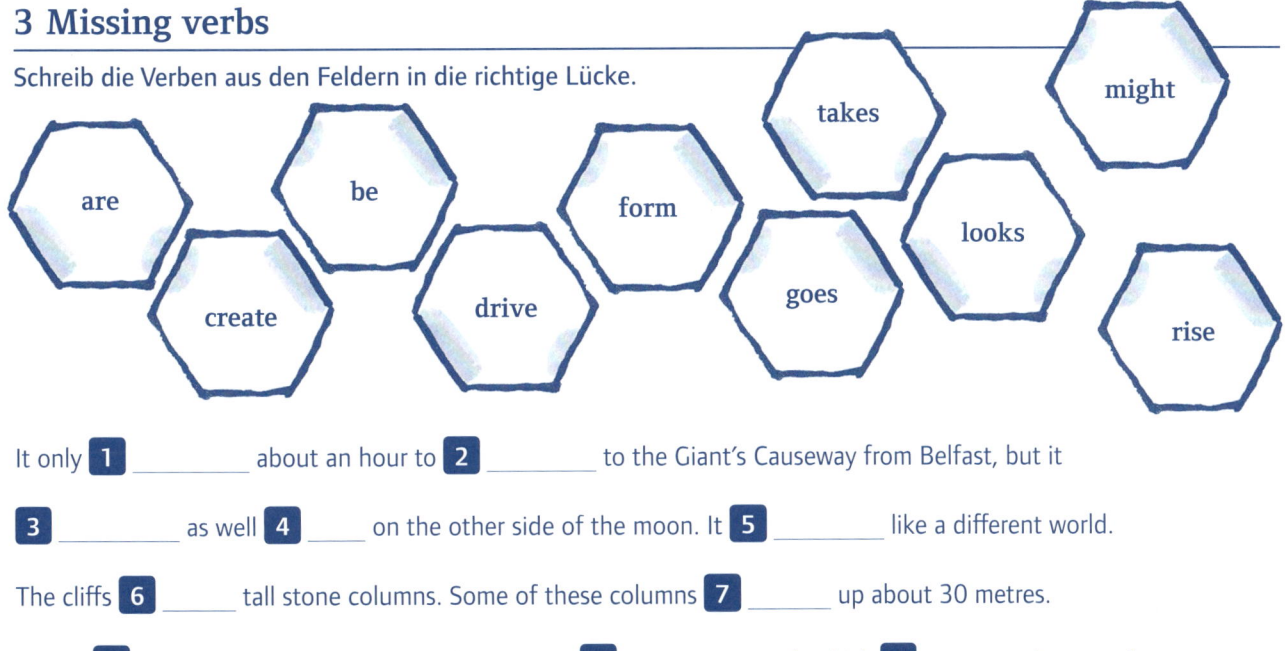

are · be · create · drive · form · takes · goes · looks · might · rise

It only **1** _____ about an hour to **2** _____ to the Giant's Causeway from Belfast, but it

3 _____ as well **4** _____ on the other side of the moon. It **5** _____ like a different world.

The cliffs **6** _____ tall stone columns. Some of these columns **7** _____ up about 30 metres.

Others **8** _____ the impression of steps that **9** _____ a path which **10** _____ down to the sea.

4 More missing verbs

Schreib die Wörter aus den Feldern in die richtige Lücke.

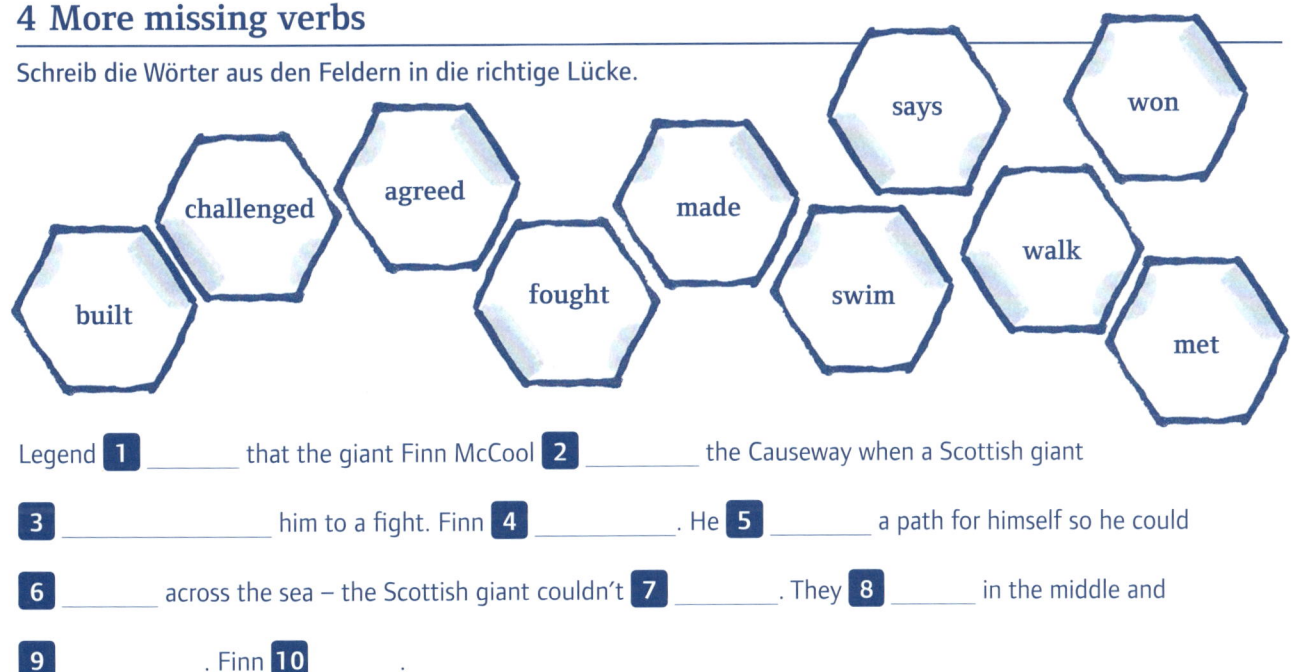

built · challenged · agreed · fought · made · swim · says · won · walk · met

Legend **1** _____ that the giant Finn McCool **2** _____ the Causeway when a Scottish giant

3 _____ him to a fight. Finn **4** _____ . He **5** _____ a path for himself so he could

6 _____ across the sea – the Scottish giant couldn't **7** _____ . They **8** _____ in the middle and

9 _____ . Finn **10** _____ .

5 Words and phrases → (p. 68)

*Not all the EU uses the euro.
And four countries which are not in the
EU use it. Do you know which?

1 We crossed the _____ in the morning. | Wir haben die **Grenze** am Morgen überquert.

2 We didn't need to _____ money. | Wir mussten kein Geld **umtauschen**.

3 The _____ of the ____ is the _____.* | Die **Währung** in der **EU** ist der **Euro**.

4 There are 100 _____ in one euro. | 100 **Cent** sind ein Euro.

5 Your _____ shows who you are. | Dein **Personalausweis** zeigt, wer du bist.

6 Where is the main building of the United _____? | Wo ist das Hauptgebäude der Vereinten **Nationen**?**

7 Britain doesn't have ID cards, just _____. | Großbritannien hat keine Ausweise, sondern **Pässe**.

8 We all want _____. _____ is terrible. | Wir wollen alle **Frieden**. **Krieg** ist furchtbar.

9 Where's the nearest _____ _____? | Wo ist die nächste **Polizeiwache**?

10 What's the _____ of France? | Wie groß ist die **Bevölkerung** von Frankreich?

11 Let's ask the _____ of the _____! | Lass uns den **Präsidenten** der **Republik** fragen!

12 How many member _____ does the EU have? | Wie viele Mitglieds**staaten** hat die EU?

13 Do you need a _____ to go there? | Muss man ein **Visum** haben, um dahin zu fahren?

14 Poor Amy! Her _____ has been _____. | Arme Amy! Ihr **Haustier** wurde **gestohlen**.

15 Dad needs to go to the _____ tomorrow. | Papa muss morgen zur **Bank**.

**It's in New York City.

6 Define the words

Vervollständige die Definitionen der Wörter.

1	**president**	the most important person in a _____
2	**border**	the line where two _____ meet
3	**population**	the _____ of _____ who live in a country
4	**war**	when countries _____
5	**pet**	an _____ which lives with a _____
6	**passport**	a little book that people show when cross a _____
7	**bank**	a place that looks after people's _____
8	**cent**	There are 100 of these in a _____.

7 Words and phrases ➜ (p. 69)

1 Every group needs a good _____.	Jede Gruppe braucht einen guten **Koordinator**.
2 The _____ of the brochure is not very nice.	Die **Gestaltung** der Broschüre ist nicht sehr schön.
3 The _____ didn't do a very good job, I think.	Der **Redakteur** hat nicht gut gearbeitet, denke ich.
4 I did a lot of _____ last week.	Ich habe letzte Woche viel **Recherche** betrieben.
5 I'm not happy with the _____ of my work.	Ich bin mit dem **Ergebnis** meiner Arbeit nicht glücklich.
6 I _____ that I do it again.	Ich **schlage vor**, es noch einmal zu tun.
7 We had a _____ about computer games.	Wir hatten eine **Diskussion** über Computerspiele.
8 I made notes on our _____.	Ich habe mir Notizen zu unserer **Entscheidung** gemacht.

8 -er or -or?

Vervollständige die Wörter mit *-er* oder *-or*.

1 The act____ showed his ID card when he got to the bord____.

2 Uncle Bob was a doct____. Then he became the direct____ of a big company.

3 The edit____ wanted more pictures in the brochure for the visit____s.

4 Chris is a good coordinat____. That's why she is the lead____ of the group.

5 Was life bett____ for our ancest____s?

6 I think I would like to be a sail____ more than a soldi____.

9 Wrong!

Finde einen Schreibfehler in jedem Satz und schreib das richtige Wort rechts auf.

1 The policeman asked to see our pasports.   _____

2 We need to do some reserch for our homework.   _____

3 What shall we do tomorrow? That's a difficult decission.   _____

4 We hope the war will end. We all want piece.   _____

5 Will Britain be a republik when the Queen dies?   _____

10 Words and phrases → (pp. 70–73)

1 _____ live in _____.	**Engel** leben im **Himmel**.
2 That's what they said in the _____ on Sunday.	Das haben sie am Sonntag im **Gottesdienst** gesagt.
3 This video is cool. _____ it _____.	Dieses Video ist cool. **Schau** es **dir an**.
4 He said no, and she _____ _____: "Why not?"	Er hat nein gesagt, und sie **so**: „Warum nicht?"
5 I want to get a _____ when I'm older.	Ich möchte ein **Motorrad** haben, wenn ich älter bin.
6 Does your dad wear a _____ at work?	Trägt dein Vater einen **Anzug** bei der Arbeit?
7 Does your grandfather _____ a _____?	**Raucht** dein Großvater **Pfeife**?
8 It looks _____ it's going to rain.	Es sieht aus, **als ob** es regnen wird.
9 Do you believe in heaven and _____?	Glaubst du an Himmel und **Hölle**?
10 I have to be home ____ 11 tonight.	Ich muss heute **bis spätestens** 23 Uhr zu Hause sein.
11 I _____ ___ _____ every morning.	Ich **dusche mich** jeden Morgen.
12 I like traditional music more than _____.	Ich mag traditionelle Musik mehr als **elektronische**.
13 Is the _____ the biggest ocean?	Ist der **Atlantik** der größte Ozean?
14 I missed the _____ of the film.	Ich habe den **Anfang** des Films verpasst.
15 So ____ _____ _____ I didn't understand it.	Deswegen habe ich ihn **zuerst** nicht verstanden.
16 Is he a _____ at this hotel, or does he work here?	Ist er **Gast** in diesem Hotel oder arbeitet er hier?
17 Her _____ _____ shows she's sad.	Ihr **Gesichtsausdruck** zeigt, dass sie traurig ist.
18 How important is _____ with people?	Wie wichtig ist der **Umgang** mit Leuten?

11 Word partners

Verbinde die Teile so, dass sie sinnvolle Paare bilden.

take · change · wear · have · explore · keep · check · rise · lie · smoke

place · a shower · down · money · a new place · a suit · a pipe · something out · up · notes

12 Words and phrases → *(p. 74)*

1 The room was prepared before my _____.

Das Zimmer wurde vor meiner **Ankunft** vorbereitet.

2 Lots of _____ things happened.

Viele **seltsame** Dinge sind passiert.

3 My first _____ was on the beach on a pony.

Mein erster **Ritt** war am Strand – mit einem Pony.

4 I'm lucky that I'm still _____.

Ich habe Glück, dass ich noch **am Leben** bin.

5 I had an _____ with my horse.

Ich hatte eine **Auseinandersetzung** mit meinem Pferd.

6 I won't _____ that horse, I'm sure!

Das Pferd werde ich nicht **vermissen**, da bin ich sicher.

7 People _____ _____ don't talk much.

Die Leute **hier in der Gegend** reden nicht viel.

8 They _____ at guests when they arrive.

Sie **starren** die Gäste **an**, wenn sie ankommen.

9 We should always _____ _____ animals.

Wir sollten Tiere immer **wichtig nehmen**.

10 I _____ _____ what you do!

Mir ist es egal, was du tust.

11 I _____ _____ – let's eat!

Ich **habe einen Riesenhunger** – lass uns essen.

12 Let's _____ the shopping after our meal.

Lass uns nach dem Essen die Einkäufe **auspacken**.

13 Oh _____ – I haven't bought any food!

Oh **Gott** – ich habe nichts zu essen gekauft!

14 I _____ people who shout a lot.

Ich **kann** Leute **nicht leiden**, die viel schreien.

13 Broken words

Verbinde die Wortteile im Rätsel und vervollständige die Sätze mit den Wörtern.

el   we   ronic

ving   ival   gu   un   ed   like   me   arr

sult   star

dis   ar   ird   pack   ice   ial   fac   nt   ect   re   serv

1 When we got home I _____ my bags.

2 I'm not hungry, I'm _____!

3 I don't like or _____ coffee. I just don't drink it.

4 She looks strange and wears _____ clothes.

5 Every time I talk to him we have an _____.

6 We clean the room before the guests' _____.

7 Is the dictionary you use _____?

8 Do you know the _____ of the match?

9 His _____ expression told me he was hungry.

10 They went to the _____ in the church.

14 Words and phrases ➔ *(pp. 75–77)*

1 What was that? I heard a loud _____.	Was war das? Ich habe einen lauten **Knall** gehört.
2 She's got a nice _____ _____.	Sie hat einen netten **regionalen Akzent**.
3 _____ English is easier to understand.	**Standard**englisch ist einfacher zu verstehen.
4 He and I are _____ and _____.	Er und ich, wir sind **Freund** und **Freundin**.
5 First, I'd like to _____ you _____ the hotel.	Zuerst möchte ich Sie **im** Hotel **willkommen heißen**.
6 Time _____ slowly when you feel bored.	Die Zeit **vergeht** langsam, wenn man sich langweilt.
7 So, where are we going _____?	Also, was machen wir **als Nächstes**?
8 We're going to Spain at _____.	Wir fahren zu **Ostern** nach Spanien.
9 Be careful, this is a busy _____.	Vorsicht, das ist eine belebte **Kreuzung**.
10 A _____ is waiting to cross the road.	Ein **Fußgänger** wartet, um die Straße zu überqueren.

15 The fourth word

Vervollständige die Lücken mit einem passenden Wort.

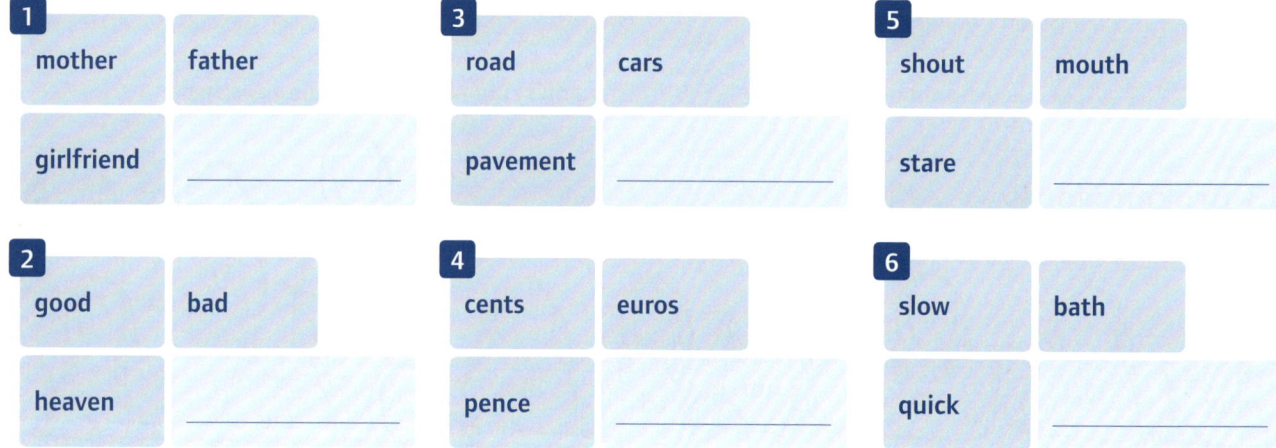

1
mother	father
girlfriend	_____

3
road	cars
pavement	_____

5
shout	mouth
stare	_____

2
good	bad
heaven	_____

4
cents	euros
pence	_____

6
slow	bath
quick	_____

16 Join the parts

Verbinde die beiden Teile der Sätze.

1 The time passed quickly

2 He's got a regional accent

3 I think some people care too much

4 In my opinion, it's not polite

5 We normally go on holiday

a about money.

b to stare at people.

c at Easter.

d because we were so busy.

e but he's easy to understand.

17 Words and phrases → *(p. 77)*

1 I often _____ the dog in the park.	Ich **führe** den Hund oft im Park **aus**.
2 Yesterday a boy tried to _____ the dog!	Gestern versuchte ein Junge, den Hund zu **treten**!
3 Then he _____ out of the park.	Dann ist er aus dem Park **gerast**.
4 Cars stop when the _____ are red.	Die Autos halten an, wenn die **Ampel** rot ist.
5 There's a lot of _____ today.	Heute ist viel **Verkehr**.
6 We have to wait until lights _____ green.	Wir müssen warten, bis die Ampel grün **wird**.
7 That's not a car; it's a _____.	Das ist doch kein Auto; es ist ein **Lieferwagen**.
8 I feel sick if I _____ _____.	Mir wird schlecht, wenn ich **mich im Kreis drehe**.
9 Some people who drive well can't _____.	Manche, die gut fahren, können nicht ein**parken**.
10 The phone rang. I answered _____.	Das Telefon klingelte. Ich ging **sofort** ran.
11 I can hear the police _____.	Ich kann die Polizei**sirene** hören.
12 Where are they? _____ they _____?	Wo sind sie? **Sind** sie **weg**?

18 Scrambled story

Verbinde die Texte so, dass sie eine Geschichte ergeben.

A My dad told me a story about something he saw in town

D walking his dog. The man shouted at the dog, and then he

G yesterday. He was in his van and he was waiting at the

B junction. Anyway, he was waiting for the lights to turn

C siren. The man heard it too, and immediately he spun

E around and raced in the opposite direction – without his dog.

J about animals. A few seconds later he heard a police

F traffic lights in the town centre. As you know, it's a very busy

H kicked it. My dad thought that was terrible, because he cares

I green when he looked into the park and saw a man who was

Answer: $\boxed{A}$ ◯ ◯ ◯ ◯ ◯ ◯ ◯

19 Words and phrases → (p. 78)

→ (p. 78)

*Another word for "people".

1 _____ _____ us can speak Italian.	**Keiner von** uns kann Italienisch sprechen.
2 I know ___ _____ _____ words in Spanish.	Ich kenne **ein paar** Wörter auf Spanisch.
3 The _____* I visited were really friendly.	Die **Leute**, die ich besuchte, waren sehr freundlich.
4 There's a lovely _____ of trees behind our house.	Hinter unserem Haus gibt es eine schöne **Reihe** Bäume.
5 He looked unhappy. "_____" I asked.	Er sah unglücklich aus. „**Was ist los?**" fragte ich.
6 We were on a _____ through the forest.	Wir waren auf einem **Pfad** durch den Wald.
7 "I'm bored," he _____.	„Ich langweile mich," **seufzte** er.
8 What do you want to do, _____ _____ you're alone?	Was willst du machen, **jetzt wo** du alleine bist?
9 The ground was _____ after the rain.	Der Boden war **rutschig** nach dem Regen.
10 I nearly fell into a _____.	Ich bin fast in einen **Graben** gefallen.

20 The right words

Kreise die richtigen Wörter ein, um die Sätze zu vervollständigen.

1 I only know (a) • **the** • **few** couple of words in French.

2 Why has the traffic stopped? What's **in** • **about** • **up** ?

3 Shall we go and explore the area, now **there** • **then** • **that** we are here.

4 Because of his accent, I understood none **from** • **of** • **about** his questions.

5 I can't stay long. I have to be home **by** • **since** • **in** two o'clock today.

6 Here is a postcard of the town in the old **years** • **weeks** • **days** .

7 They had an accident. They are lucky to be **living** • **alive** • **live** .

8 I asked him to help and he was **say** • **go** • **like** "Why?"

9 We need to buy more coffee. There's not much **leave** • **left** • **less** .

10 There's nothing to see here. We might **as** • **so** • **very** well go home now.

21 Words and phrases ➜ *(p. 79)*

1 Life was different _____.	Das Leben war **früher** anders.
2 We stopped to look at a _____.	Wir hielten an, um einen **Grabstein** anzuschauen.
3 Lots of people are _____ here.	Viele Menschen liegen hier **begraben**.
4 They died of _____ or _____.	Sie sind an **Hungersnot** oder **Krankheit** gestorben.
5 Many people _____ to America.	Viele Leute **sind** nach Amerika **ausgewandert**.
6 The _____ did nothing to help them.	Die **Regierung** hat nichts gemacht, um ihnen zu helfen.
7 19% of Ireland's _____ go to the USA.	19% von Irlands **Exporten** gehen in die USA.
8 We stopped at the _____.	Wir hielten am **Bach** an.
9 Pipes smell nice, but pipe _____ smells awful.	Pfeifen riechen gut, aber Pfeifen**asche** riecht furchtbar.
10 I'm _____ he isn't talking about _____.	Ich bin **froh**, dass er nicht über den **Tod** redet.
11 I love it here, _____ when it's sunny.	Ich liebe es hier, **vor allem** wenn es sonnig ist.
12 We could live here – that's a nice _____.	Wir könnten hier wohnen – das ist ein netter **Gedanke**.

18 True or false

Sind die Aussagen wahr oder falsch?

	True	False
1 When something has burned, you can see ashes.	◯	◯
2 A headache is a disease.	◯	◯
3 A stream is normally bigger than a river.	◯	◯
4 Famines happen when people don't have enough food to live.	◯	◯
5 People who emigrate go to live in another country.	◯	◯
6 It is normal to bury people when they are alive.	◯	◯
7 A bang is louder than a sigh.	◯	◯
8 If something is slippery, it is normally dry.	◯	◯
9 Exports are things you produce then sell in another country.	◯	◯
10 A trail is the same as a road.	◯	◯
11 If you ask "What's up?", you want to know the time.	◯	◯
12 The Atlantic is between Europe and America.	◯	◯

Extraordinary Scotland

1 Words and phrases → *(pp. 82–83)*

1 We heard an _____ sound. — Wir hörten ein **außergewöhnliches** Geräusch.

2 This film ____ _____ Scotland. — Der Film **macht Werbung für** Schottland.

3 Somebody was playing the _____. — Jemand hat **Dudelsack** gespielt.

4 _____! Your chair is going to break. — **Achtung**! Dein Stuhl wird bald kaputtgehen.

5 She's _____ ____ a contest. — Sie **nimmt an** einem Wettbewerb **teil**.

6 I'd like to watch some _____ _____. — Ich möchte ein **Turnier** für **Hütehunde** anschauen.

7 The _____ are a beautiful part of Scotland. — Das **Hochland** ist ein schöner Teil von Schottland.

8 I was _____ my uncle's _____. — Ich war **an Bord der Jacht** meines Onkels.

9 It's a _____ boat and very sweet. — Es ist ein **kleines** Boot und sehr süß.

10 We visited the _____ of Heligoland. — Wir besuchten die **Insel** Helgoland.

11 How do you _____ different _____? — Wie **identifiziert** man verschiedene **Delfine**?

12 I use lots of _____ _____. — Ich verwende viele **soziale Medien**.

13 He doesn't use the internet. He's _____. — Er benutzt das Internet nicht. Er ist **ungewöhnlich**.

14 Really? Young people _____ love it. Wirklich? — **Üblich**erweise lieben es die jungen Leute.

2 Friends

Verbinde die Wörter, die zueinander passen.

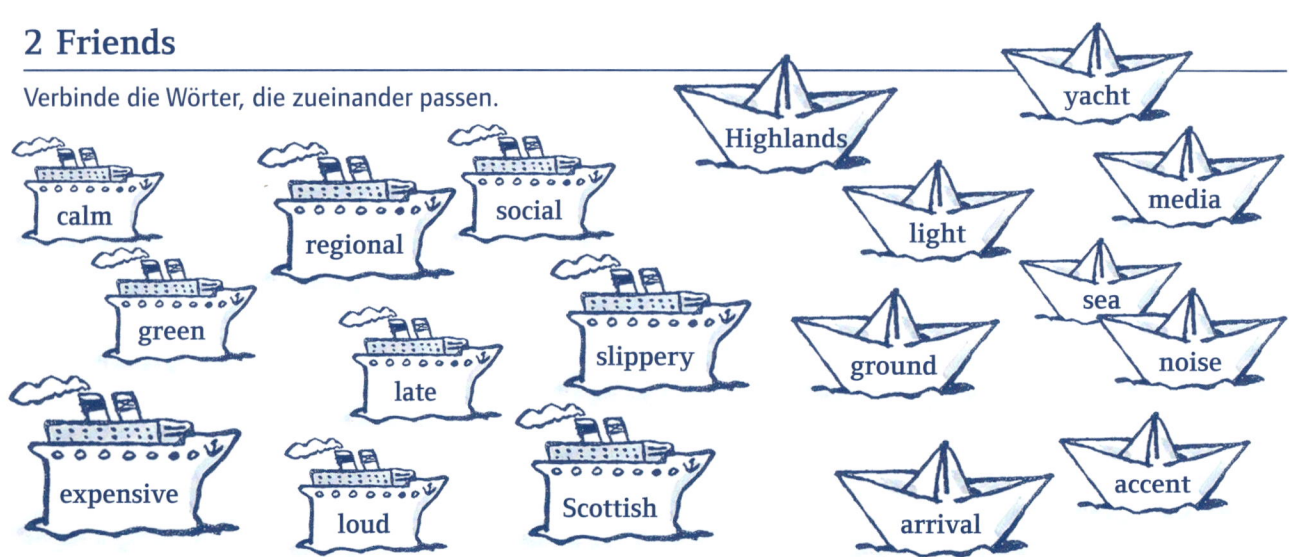

3 Match the parts

Verbinde die Sätze links mit den Aussagen rechts.

1 It's a very unusual film.

2 Do you play a musical instrument?

3 It was a very successful event.

4 Do the police know the man who did this?

5 They have a house in Scotland, I think.

6 Are they going to the trials this weekend?

7 They go everywhere with their dog.

8 Did you hear about what happened to him?

9 That looks dangerous.

10 Is that their yacht?

A Yes, look out!

B Yes, in the Highlands.

C Yes, usually.

D Yes, the bagpipes.

E Yes, it's extraordinary.

F Yes, on social media.

G Yes, they're on board now.

H Yes, they promoted it well.

I Yes, they have identified him.

J Yes, they're competing on Sunday.

What's wrong with these dolphins?

4 The right pair

Vervollständige jeden Satz dieser Geschichte mit dem richtigen Paar Wörter.

on + out

with + on

on + of

to + by

after + at

in + for

about + to

of + to

about + in

for + in

1 Did you hear *about* my trip _____ Scotland?

2 I went there _____ a week _____ the holidays.

3 _____ some friends, I even did some research _____ dolphins.

4 We were _____ a yacht near the Isle _____ Barra.

5 Scientists don't know much _____ the dolphins that live _____ the sea there.

6 Dolphins get caught _____ fishing nets, and pollution is also a problem _____ them.

7 We learned _____ identify the dolphins _____ their dorsal fins.

8 We took photos _____ the dolphins _____ help us do that.

9 It was my first time _____ board a boat. We went _____ on the water every day.

10 You have to look _____ yourself _____ sea – it can be dangerous, you know.

5 Words and phrases → (p. 84)

1 Our teacher asked for a _____ .

Unser Lehrer hat nach einem **Freiwilligen** gefragt.

2 There are often whale _____ here.

Es gibt hier oft **Sichtungen** von Walen.

3 I _____ my _____ ____ when I know the answer.

Ich **melde mich**, wenn ich die Antwort weiß.

4 We can _____ the _____ .

Wir können die **Verschmutzung fotografieren**.

5 It's good to _____ _____ in the fresh air.

Es ist gut, **Zeit** in der frischen Luft zu **verbringen**.

6 I _____ too much _____ last week.

Ich habe letzte Woche zu viel **Geld ausgegeben**.

7 We need to _____ wild animals.

Wir müssen die wilden Tiere **schützen**.

8 Your dad is a teacher: where does he _____ ?

Dein Vater ist Lehrer: Wo **unterrichtet** er?

9 Each dolphin has a different _____ ____ .

Jeder Delfin hat eine andere **Rückenflosse**.

6 Quiz questions

Schreibe die Antwort auf die Fragen rechts auf.

1 What do you call someone who offers to help or do something? _____

2 What is the name for a small island? _____

3 Which part of a dolphin can you see when they swim in the sea? _____

4 What's another word for "take pictures with a camera"? _____

5 What should you do if you want to ask a question in class? _____

6 What causes bad quality air, land and water? _____

7 What verb goes with "time" and "money"? _____

8 What is the name of Scotland's national musical instrument? _____

7 The right words

Kreise die richtigen Wörter ein, um die Sätze zu vervollständigen.

1 There were many **sights** · (**sightings of**) · **from** big cats in the Highlands.

2 We **spend** · **spent** a day in the city seeing the **sights** · **sightings** .

3 My parents **teach** · **taught** me how to cook **as** · **when** I was younger.

4 I can **teach** · **taught** you how to **photograph** · **photo** the animals.

8 Words and phrases → *(pp. 84–86)*

1 You need to _____ everything you see. — Du musst alles **dokumentieren**, was du siehst.

2 Can you find our _____ on the map? — Kannst du unseren **Standort** auf der Karte finden?

3 We always _____ changes in the weather. — Wir **überwachen** immer Wetterveränderungen.

4 He said "no" with a _____ of his head. — Er sagte mit einer Kopf**bewegung** „nein".

5 The sea is too _____ to swim today. — Zum Schwimmen ist das Meer heute zu **stürmisch**.

6 Even when it is _____ I get _____. — Auch wenn es **ruhig** ist, werde ich **seekrank**.

7 Where do you _____ the sugar? — Wo **bewahrst** du den Zucker **auf**?

8 I _____ a piece of pizza for you. — Ich **habe** ein Stück Pizza für dich **aufgehoben**.

9 I just want to _____ for a while. — Ich will **mich** einfach eine Weile **ausruhen**.

10 Many people want to _____ from Africa. — Viele Leute wollen aus Afrika **fliehen**.

11 We read about the _____ in the paper. — Wir lasen in der Zeitung über die **Flucht**.

12 Our new TV has a _____ _____. — Unser neuer Fernseher hat eine **Bildschirmteilung**.

9 Match the sentences

Verbinde die Sätze mit einer ähnlichen Bedeutung.

1 I'm not good on boats and yachts.

2 It's very rough today.

3 It's much smaller than a river.

4 She taught me everything that I know about it.

5 I was working all day today.

6 He escapes to the country whenever he can.

7 I went away with a couple of friends.

8 I keep the coffee here.

9 They record the situation every day.

10 That is quite unusual.

A I learned it all from her.

B I haven't had time to relax.

C They are monitoring how things change.

D It was me and two or three others.

E It doesn't often happen.

F I get seasick.

G It was much calmer yesterday.

H He gets out of the city as often as possible.

I It's just a stream.

J This is where I put it.

10 Words and phrases ➜ (p. 88)

1 What is my _____ to go on stage?	Was ist mein **Stichwort**, um auf die Bühne zu gehen?
2 I'm sorry. It was my _____.	Tut mir leid. Es war meine **Schuld**.
3 I was just waiting _____.	Ich habe einfach **hinter der Bühne** gewartet.
4 But it's no problem. It was just a _____.	Aber das ist kein Problem. Es war bloß eine **Probe**.
5 I can say this to you, but ____ _____ _____.	Ich kann dir das sagen, aber **niemandem sonst**.
6 I'm finding it hard to _____.	Ich finde es schwer, **mich** zu **konzentrieren**.
7 My teacher always _____ _____ me.	Mein Lehrer **hackt** immer **auf** mir **herum**.
8 I _____ _____ _____ his silly jokes.	Ich **habe** seine blöden Witze **satt**.
9 What _____ was Schalke at the end of the year?	Welchen **Platz** hatte Schalke am Ende des Jahres?

11 True or false?

Sind die Aussagen wahr oder falsch?

	True	False
1 Most people find it hard to concentrate when it is very noisy.	◯	◯
2 Cues tell actors where and when to do something.	◯	◯
3 The audience sit backstage in a theatre.	◯	◯
4 When you say you are tired of something, it means you want to go to bed.	◯	◯
5 Cows and horses have fins.	◯	◯
6 A rehearsal is a sort of practice for actors and musicians.	◯	◯
7 A split screen is a screen which is broken.	◯	◯

12 The fourth word

Vervollständige die Lücken mit einem vierten Wort.

1

usual	unusual
polite	_____

2

day	night
war	_____

3

decide	decision
move	_____

4

van	drive
horse	_____

5

hand	hit
foot	_____

6

live	die
life	_____

13 Words and phrases ➜ *(pp. 89–91)*

1 This exercise is really _____ . Diese Aufgabe ist echt **knallhart**.

2 Someone in the crowd _____ _____ my _____ . Jemand in der Menge **trat** mir **auf die Zehen**.

3 Mum _____ me ___ _____ _____ today. Mama **machte** mir heute **das Leben schwer**.

4 I needed 30 minutes to _____ _____ . Ich brauchte 30 Minuten, **mich** wieder zu **beruhigen**.

5 I gave the police a _____ of the man. Ich gab der Polizei eine **Beschreibung** des Mannes ab.

6 "I like you" is an example of _____ speech. „Ich mag dich" ist ein Beispiel für **direkte** Rede.

7 Adults can go out _____ they like. Erwachsene dürfen ausgehen, **wann immer** sie wollen.

8 _____ you want, do it! **Egal was** du willst, tu es!

9 Not all _____ for social media are the same. Nicht alle **Plattformen** für soziale Medien sind gleich.

10 Loriot was the best German _____ ever. Loriot war der allerbeste **Komiker** Deutschlands.

11 What _____ is there here? Was für **Unterhaltung** gibt es hier?

12 What really _____ me is live music. Das, was mich wirklich **interessiert**, ist Livemusik.

14 So much stress

Diese Wörter haben alle drei Silben. Aber wo liegt die Betonung? Schreib die Wörter in die richtige Spalte.

> Atlantic · beginning · concentrate · continue · disappear · emigrate · engineer · government · impolite · indirect · interrupt · location · motorbike · photograph · pollution · president · referee · rehearsal · slippery · volunteer · whenever

First syllabus stress ['---]	**Second syllable stress [-'--]**	**Third syllable stress [--'-]**

15 Words and phrases → *(pp. 92–93)*

1 Our teacher gave us a _____ about Scotland.   Unser Lehrer gab uns einen **Handzettel** über Schottland.

2 Then he showed us a _____.   Dann zeigte er uns eine **Folie**.

3 It was a picture of a _____ in a forest.   Es war ein Foto eines **Luchs** im Wald.

4 We talked about _____ and their _____.   Wir redeten über **Luchse** und ihren **Lebensraum**.

5 In the winter, the lynx has a thick, silky _____.   Im Winter hat der Luchs ein dickes, seidiges **Fell**.

6 It's a very successful _____.   Er ist ein sehr erfolgreiches **Raubtier**.

7 Like us, the lynx is a _____.   Wie wir ist der Luchs ein **Säugetier**.

8 Most animals try to protect their _____.   Die meisten Tiere versuchen, ihr **Revier** zu schützen.

9 What's the main _____ of a good presentation?   Was ist das Haupt**element** einer guten Präsentation?

10 – Practice: it's always _____.   – Die Übung: Sie ist immer **nötig**.

16 Broken words

Verbinde die Wortteile zu Wörtern und vervollständige mit ihnen den Text.

Our teacher gave us a **1** _____ about wild animals in Scotland. We learned about wild cats and lynxes,

and their **2** _____. They are **3** _____, which means they kill and eat other animals.

They have a thick **4** _____ to keep them warm, which is **5** _____ because they live in a cold place.

We learned that animals have a **6** _____, which is the area where they live. They will

fight to **7** _____ it – and their babies. **8** _____ are like us: they are **9** _____.

For homework we had to make a **10** _____ about the life of wild animals.

17 Words and phrases ➔ (p. 94)

1 _____ : Black and white cat.	**VERMISST**: Schwarzweiße Katze.
2 I love the colour of the _____ .	Ich liebe die Farbe des **Heidekrauts**.
3 I was up on the moor. The sea was _____ .	Ich war oben auf dem Hochmoor. Das Meer war **darunter**.
4 The sky _____ was blue.	Der Himmel **darüber** war blau.
5 There was some _____ before the contest.	Es gab etwas **Anspannung** vor dem Wettberwerb.
6 I heard a loud _____ and the race started.	Ich hörte einen lauten **Pfiff**, und das Rennen fing an.
7 I looked ____ _____ as the car left the road.	Ich schaute **entsetzt** zu, als das Auto die Straße verließ.
8 There was a terrible _____ .	Es gab ein furchtbares **Geräusch**.
9 I _____ _____ and took a glass …	Ich **streckte die Hand aus** und nahm ein Glas, …
10 … because I was thirsty. My throat was _____ .	… weil ich Durst hatte. Meine Kehle war **trocken**.
11 Do you think Arsenal will _____ Bayern?	Meinst du, Arsenal wird Bayern **besiegen**?
12 I know you well. I can _____ your _____ .	Ich kenne dich gut. Ich kann deine **Gedanken lesen**.
13 _____ work in the fresh air a lot.	**Schäfer** arbeiten viel an der frischen Luft.

18 Rhymes

Welche zwei Wörter in jeder Zeile reimen sich? Schreib sie rechts auf.

1 below · now · go · do _____ _____

2 dry · stay · high · bury _____ _____

3 above · tough · laugh · stuff _____ _____

4 noise · nose · boys · tries _____ _____

5 lynx · thick · banks · thinks _____ _____

6 tread · made · afraid · weird _____ _____

7 taught · boat · thought · throat _____ _____

8 cue · move · rough · through _____ _____

9 late · compete · might · beat _____ _____

10 came · calm · farm · storm _____ _____

19 Words and phrases ➜ *(pp. 94–96)*

1 They go to New York every year – I'm _____. | Sie fahren jedes Jahr nach New York – ich bin **neidisch**.

2 I _____ it when you say that. | Ich **hasse** es, wenn du das sagst.

3 I heard the news and _____ _____ _____. | Ich hörte die Nachricht und **brach in Tränen aus**.

4 The trees were moving _____ in the wind. | Die Bäume bewegten sich **sanft** im Wind.

5 "I'm _____," he said as she _____. | „Ich bin **wach**", sagte er, als sie **klopfte**.

6 The village has a _____ to the dead soldiers. | Das Dorf hat ein **Denkmal** für die gefallenen Soldaten.

7 The team is _____ now. | Die Mannschaft ist jetzt **auf dem zweiten Platz**.

20 Word fields

Schreib die Wörter von den Mauersteinen ins passende Wortfeld.

Atlantic | bang | border | career | computer | dolphin | editor | glad | habitat | hate | horror | jealous | knock | life jacket | local | miss | northern | office | on board | platform | regional | screen | send | shepherd | sigh | siren | suit | text | whistle | yacht

Sea

Place

Feelings

Work

Noise

Social media

21 Scrambled story

Verbinde die Zeilen so, dass sie eine Geschichte ergeben.

A Here are some pictures of my trip to Scotland. I went there last summer. We

G castle and other sights, like churches with old gravestones. A festival was

E visa or passport when you get to the border. They use the same currency, too:

B pounds and pence. We stayed in Edinburgh for a couple of days and saw the

C were playing were all wearing those skirts, you know, they call them

D to understand what people said because of the regional accent

H but I didn't find it difficult. One woman told us about when she was a "wee"

F events, and we heard lots of people playing the bagpipes:

I drove there from London. It's a different country, but you don't need a

J taking place there at the same time. We saw a couple of interesting

K girl. That means when she was little. Next we went north to see the Highlands.

M kilts. Some friends gave me a warning that it might be a challenge

L the music is traditional, and the noise is extraordinary. The men who

22 Missing words

Vervollständige die Sätze mit zwei Wörtern aus der rechten Spalte.

1 I'm _____. Is there somewhere to get some food _____ here?   **busy · starving · round**

2 The photos in the _____ give a good _____ of the city.   **brochure · impression · location**

3 He was tired, so I _____ that he should have a _____.   **spread · suggested · shower**

4 Someone _____ on the door. Immediately, I was fully _____.   **bang · knocked · awake**

5 The boy _____ into tears when the bully _____ on his toes.   **broke · burst · trod**

6 Dad gave me a _____ time because I forgot to _____ the dog.   **walk · strong · hard**

7 Can you _____ the colours of the _____?   **call · rainbow · name**

8 There's no _____ of anyone here. They're _____.   **notice · sign · gone**

9 The _____ wasn't real. We were _____.   **argument · pollution · pretending**

10 She gave me some _____ advice about my _____.   **translation · practical · natural**

23 Crossword

Vervollständige die Sätze und trag die Lösungen in das Kreuzworträtsel ein.

Across →

2 It wasn't easy. It was a big ▇▇▇ for me.

3 We waited for the traffic light to ▇▇▇ green.

6 Careful. The pavement is ▇▇▇ because of the rain.

8 We need more milk. There isn't any ▇▇▇ .

12 I went to the cinema with a ▇▇▇ of friends.

13 I felt sick because the sea was very ▇▇▇ .

14 My dad drives a ▇▇▇ for work.

16 Life was very different ▇▇▇ the old days.

17 We've nearly finished. What shall we do ▇▇▇ ?

20 We have a dog as a ▇▇▇ .

22 He was very tall. He was a ▇▇▇ .

23 The car drove into the ▇▇▇ at the side.

24 I'm thirsty. My throat is very ▇▇▇ .

Down ↓

1 When shall we ▇▇▇ tonight? 8 pm?

4 Please walk more slowly and don't ▇▇▇ .

5 Relax! ▇▇▇ down!

7 He always says "please" and "thanks". He's very ▇▇▇ .

9 The ▇▇▇ around here are very friendly.

10 The ▇▇▇ of Britain is over 58 million.

11 It's not a true story. I made it ▇▇▇ .

15 It's broken, but I didn't do it. It's not my ▇▇▇ .

18 My mum ▇▇▇ me how to cook last summer.

19 They danced and started to ▇▇▇ round.

21 Have the police identified the dead ▇▇▇ they found?

Enjoy your summer holidays and see you soon!